OXFORD PLAYSCRIPTS

FLESH AND BLOOD

Benjamin Hulme-Cross

Also includes 'The Body Snatcher'
by Robert Louis Stevenson

T0346715

OXFORD
UNIVERSITY PRESS

OXFORD
UNIVERSITY PRESS

Great Clarendon Street, Oxford, OX2 6DP,
United Kingdom

Oxford University Press is a department of the University of Oxford.
It furthers the University's objective of excellence in research, scholarship,
and education by publishing worldwide. Oxford is a registered trade mark of Oxford
University Press in the UK and in certain other countries

Flesh and Blood © Benjamin Hulme-Cross 2014
Activities section © Oxford University Press 2014

The moral rights of the author have been asserted

First published in 2014

All rights reserved. No part of this publication may be reproduced, stored in a retrieval
system, or transmitted, in any form or by any means, without the prior permission in
writing of Oxford University Press, or as expressly permitted by law, by licence or under
terms agreed with the appropriate reprographics rights organization. Enquiries concerning
reproduction outside the scope of the above should be sent to the Rights Department,
Oxford University Press, at the address above.

You must not circulate this work in any other form
and you must impose this same condition on any acquirer

All rights whatsoever in this play are strictly reserved and application for performance
should strictly be made for commencement of rehearsal to: Rights Department,
Education Division, Oxford University Press, Great Clarendon Street, Oxford, OX2 6DP.
No performance may be made unless a licence has been obtained and no alterations may
be made on the title or the text of the play without the author's prior written consent.

British Library Cataloguing in Publication Data
Data available

978 019 839350 4

12

Printed in Great Britain by CPI Group (UK) Ltd., Croydon CR0 4YY

Acknowledgements

Cover: Joshua Sheldon/Trevillion Images

Illustrations by Neil Chapman.

Photos: p70: Bettmann/CORBIS; p96: BORTEL Pavel – Pavelmidi/Shutterstock;
p111: Mary Evans Picture Library/Alamy

The Publisher would like to thank Jenny Roberts for writing the Activities section.

CONTENTS

WHAT THE PLAYWRIGHT SAYS

For many of us there is something instantly fascinating about the monster we cannot see, the beast that defies our rational beliefs. Over the centuries we have given the monster many shapes. Most well-known today are vampires, werewolves and zombies, but there are many more. Of course we know these things aren't real, but somehow we can't quite let them go.

As a child I used to deliberately scare myself. Walking through the trees at night during a camping trip I would know I was in no real danger. I would hear my friends shouting at each other in their tents. And then the seed of terror: something is out there! Something evil in the night. Something infinitely bigger than I can understand. And somehow it's reaching out for me... Neck tingling, back arched I would sprint back to the tents, jump into my sleeping bag and squeeze my eyes tight shut!

I wanted to write a play that captured some of that instinctive, toe-curling, goose-pimply fear that comes with any sense of a supernatural menace. The challenge faced by a writer of this sort of thing is to make it seem almost believable that the characters are in danger when few of us really believe in monsters. I needed something that would make you shiver but that wasn't a made-up monster. And that is where body-snatching comes in.

Body-snatching was a very real problem in the early 19th century. Medical science had developed to the point that it was essential young doctors should be trained in human anatomy. They needed precise knowledge of exactly how each muscle, sinew, bone, organ and vein worked. They could only learn this, as they do today, by dissecting human corpses. However, it was illegal for anatomists to dissect any bodies other than those belonging to executed criminals. There weren't nearly enough bodies to go around, so people started digging up recently buried corpses and selling them to anatomy schools for a tidy profit.

In the dead of night these robbers would arrive at fog-shrouded graveyards, dig down through six feet of earth, prise open a coffin and drag the fresh corpse up from the grave. Now if that isn't a toe-curling, goose-pimply setting where the idea of a supernatural menace seems a bit more real, I don't know what is!

As soon as I knew that the play was going to feature body-snatching, I pulled a book down from the shelf and re-read a classic short story by one of my heroes: 'The Body Snatcher' by Robert Louis Stevenson. What a story! There is a strong sense of tingly terror throughout. The main characters, Fettes and Macfarlane, are the young body snatchers. There is a murder and a ghost. There is the ethical debate about body-snatching – ghoulish horror on one hand, medical necessity on the other. Best of all, there is a brilliantly set up and truly haunting twist at the end.

I decided immediately that I wanted to include something of 'The Body Snatcher' in my play. And that is why, in *Flesh and Blood*, you will find murder, ghosts and two body snatchers by the names of Fettes and Macfarlane who argue about the morality of their trade. I hope that something in the final scene of the play resonates with the end of 'The Body Snatcher', but I can't say any more about that for now!

Benjamin Hulme-Cross

A Note on Staging

Setting

For the most part, scenes are set alternately in the graveyard and in a room inside the vicarage. Acts 1 and 3 are set in the present day; Act 2 in the early 19th century.

The room in the vicarage needs to look obviously different – old, faded and abandoned in the present day, light and lived in in the 19th century. Some suggestions for achieving the contrast include:

- covering present-day furniture in old shrouds/dust sheets
- brighter lighting for the 19th century
- if using any decorations on walls—for example, pictures or mirrors—these could be set at angles in the present day and straight in the 19th century.

Open graves

The opening of graves will present a challenge in some schools. Both in the vicarage and in the graveyard, it is necessary to create the impression that people can enter and emerge from a grave or the floorboards. If you have a stage with a trapdoor, or similar this will be easy. If not, you may need to consider placing the opening just out of sight offstage.

Alternatively, you may be able to block off a part of the stage so that the stage floor in that area cannot be seen. This could be done with gravestones in the graveyard, or furniture inside the vicarage.

Fighting

There are various moments when one person swings a spade at another character and misses. Care must be taken either to use a lightweight replica of a spade, or else to ensure that there is some distance between the character with the spade and the person they are attacking. It may help to avoid staging these fights side-on to the audience, so that the distance between the characters is less clear. In one case the spade connects and Eliza kills Samuel. The easiest way to negotiate this would be for Samuel to be retreating out of sight, for Eliza—still onstage—to swing the spade and for Samuel then to fall forwards back into view onstage.

Doubling

The Man and Reverend Cameron, as well as Samuel and Dr Miller, could be played by the same actors to demonstrate the connections.

COSTUMES AND PROPS

Act 1: Present day
Scene 1: A stormy graveyard, dusk
- Caitlin, Danny, Emma and Zack in outdoor gear, Zack carrying a backpack. All except Emma wearing head torches.
- Gravestones in between a gate on one side and the vicarage wall on the other side of the stage.
- Spade hidden behind the gravestone where Zack will trip.
- Some removable boards tacked over a 'window' in the wall of the vicarage. Needs to be possible to enter and exit stage through window.
- Sound effects: breaking glass, howling wind.

Scene 2: Inside the vicarage, night
- Head torches switched on until lighting improves after candles are lit.
- Chairs covered with dust sheets, heavy desk over the openable 'floorboards'.
- A wooden box containing candles, candlesticks and an old roll of paper as the news-sheet.
- Zack's backpack containing a box of matches.
- Man wearing black hat and full-length black coat with neck covered.
- Sound effects: scratching and knocking, clap of thunder.

Act 2: 19th century
Scene 1: Inside the vicarage, daylight
- 19th-century/Victorian costumes: full-length dresses for female characters, vicar's clothes for Reverend Cameron.
- The room is now bright and clean.
- Desk now out of the way against a wall, books and writing paper on it.
- Duster for Mrs Barker.

Scene 2: Graveyard at night
- Lighting from the moon or window.
- Samuel in workman's clothes.
- Gravestones positioned so that the Barker girls can be seen hiding behind them, invisible to Eliza and Samuel.

Scene 3: Inside the vicarage, daylight
- Book for Reverend Cameron to place on desk and forget.
- Broom or duster for Mrs Barker.

Scene 4: Graveyard at night

- Fettes and Macfarlane dressed in black, a lantern.
- Spade to be used in gravedigging and as weapon.
- Bags of 'earth' to be removed from grave.
- A muddy shroud.
- An actor, or dummy, as corpse wrapped in shroud.
- Coins with which Macfarlane pays Eliza.
- Blood to appear on Samuel's face after the attack.

Scene 5: Inside the vicarage, daylight

- Bag of coins for Eliza to retrieve.
- Stage set to allow Eliza to hide under the floorboards.
- Desk needs to be dragged to cover hiding place mid-scene.
- Constable Stevenson and Constable Wallace in police uniform; spectacles for Constable Stevenson.
- Sound effect: scratching, knocking and muffled cries for help.

Act 3: Present day
Scene 1: Graveyard at night

- Man with make-up on neck indicating extreme bruising from hanging.
- The spade, near to hand.

Scene 2: Inside the vicarage, night

- Desk initially covers the openable floorboards, Eliza hiding beneath.
- The spade, near to hand.
- Human skull and bones hidden beneath the floorboards.
- Zack's backpack in which to put the bones.
- Sound effect: scratching, knocking and splintering sound as floorboards thrown into air.

Act 4: Present day
Scene 1: Outside in a large garden

- Setting could just be indicated with sunlight and birdsong.
- Two chairs facing each other.
- Dr Miller in white lab coat with clipboard, or notebook and pen. Mobile phone and business cards in his pocket.
- Emma wears memorable clothes and sits with the spade against her chair.
- Eliza's clothes are identical to Emma's.
- Caitlin, in nurse's uniform, carrying a file.
- Sound effect: mobile phone ringtone.

Character List

Present-day characters

Emma Barker, 13 years old   A shy, small girl; rather frightened

Caitlin, 14 years old   Emma's feistier and older friend; tends to take charge

Zack, 13 years old   Cocky; wants to be leader of the pack but never is

Danny, 13 years old   Quite funny in a sarcastic, pessimistic way

Dr Miller, adult   Emma Barker's psychologist

19th century characters

Eliza Cameron, 16 years old   Angry, highly strung; in love with Samuel and resentful of her father

Samuel Miller, 17 years old   Village carpenter; Eliza's beau

Reverend Cameron, adult   Vicar of the parish of Caldmere

Mrs Barker, adult   The kind-hearted housekeeper in the Camerons' house

Bess Barker, 11 years old   The housekeeper's daughter

Nelly Barker, 10 years old   The housekeeper's daughter

Macfarlane, adult   A body snatcher

Fettes, adult   A body snatcher

Constable Stevenson, adult   Local constable

Constable Wallace, adult   Local constable

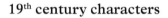

Act 1

SCENE 1

*A graveyard at twilight. There are several gravestones. On one side of the graveyard is a gate, on the other is the wall of a house with a boarded-up window and a door. A howling wind can be heard throughout this scene. Alone and afraid, as if in a dream, **Emma** walks onstage through the gate. She looks around her slowly. Lightly, she touches a gravestone.*

Emma   How can this be happening?

Caitlin walks onstage, through the gate.

Caitlin   You found us a house! Emma, you're the best! *[Then, noticing **Emma**'s strange state]* Are you OK?

10

Emma	I swear this is the place in the dreams I told you about.
Caitlin	*[Not really listening]* Hmm? Come on, let's get inside. We can talk about it there.
Emma	I really don't think that's a good idea.
Caitlin	What? We're lost. It's getting dark. We've got no reception. Look, you stay here a minute. *[Caitlin walks over to the wall of the house and calls back]* And Emma, don't worry. They're just dreams.
	Emma *continues to look slowly and wonderingly around her. From offstage, the laboured progress and shouted conversation of* ***Zack*** *and* ***Danny*** *can be heard.*
Zack	This is stupid. She doesn't have a clue where we are!
Danny	Yeah. But none of us has got any better ideas.
Zack	My dad is going to kill Mr Howard! Character-building half-term trip? Yeah right!
Danny	Shut up about your dad! *[Pause]* But yeah, this is bad. They're not going to find us in this weather.
	Danny *and* ***Zack*** *walk onstage through the gate.* Zack *is carrying a backpack.*
Zack	Emma! Have you got any idea… *[Then, seeing the house]* Oh! I knew we'd be OK.
Caitlin	Err… there's no one in there. It's all boarded up. Looks like it's been like that for ages.
Danny	So we just break in, right?
Emma	No! Guys, I really don't think we should…
Danny	Eh? We've lost the others. No adults. No one who knows how to survive outdoors for more than five minutes.
Zack	*[Coughs]* Well, actually, I do know the basics.
Danny	Shut up, Zack. Emma, we have to break in. We can't stay outside in a storm all night. We'll die.

Zack	I was just going to say, the first thing you have to do in a survival situation...
Danny and Caitlin	Shut up!
Zack	Fine, ignore me then.
Caitlin	Right, we need something to help get the boards off the windows.
Danny	Come on, let's get on with it. I'm freezing.
Zack	We're all cold, Danny.
Caitlin	Will you two just stop it!
	Emma stays where she is, staring nervously at the house, while the others walk towards it. Zack trips on something that has been concealed by one of the gravestones, and falls with a shout.
Caitlin	Are you alright?
Zack	Yeah, yeah, I'm fine. *[Sitting on the ground and picking up a spade and waving it around]* I tripped over a spade. What's that doing here?
Danny	Err, we're in a graveyard.
Zack	Thanks, I hadn't noticed.
Danny	So I guess that was the spade they used to dig the graves with.
Caitlin	Eeugh!
Danny	*[Imitating a zombie]* You could've fallen into a grave, Zack!
Caitlin	Stop it.
Zack	Hey, we can use it to break in.
Caitlin	Good idea.
	Zack stands up and shouts loudly in pain, falling over again.
Zack	I think I've broken my ankle or something.
Danny	Well, you're lame alright!

Zack	I'm serious.
Caitlin	OK… um… Emma, let's get Zack over to the house. Emma? *[Looks around and sees **Emma** still standing near the gate]* Emma, come on! Danny, you break in. Think you can manage that?
Danny	*[Sounding unsure]* Yeah, sure.
Zack	Yeah, right.
Danny	Shut up, lamo.
	Emma and Caitlin each take one of Zack's arms over their shoulders, and they all hobble over to the wall of the house. Danny takes the spade and starts jabbing away at the boarded up window. Emma wanders off.
Zack	*[After a minute]* Come on, how difficult can it be? We need to get inside. Hurry up!
Danny	Why don't you just worry about your terrible life-threatening injury?
	Zack turns away in a sulk. Danny continues knocking at the boards. Caitlin walks over to Emma who is standing centre stage, and puts an arm around her shoulders
Caitlin	Emma, relax! Nothing bad is going to happen.
Emma	So how did I know where we were?
Caitlin	I dunno, probably déjà vu or something. It doesn't mean anything.
Emma	*[Pointing at the house]* The house looks just like that, but without the boards. People live there. In the dream, I mean. I never remember who. I just wake up knowing they want to kill me.
	Emma buries her face in Caitlin's shoulder.
Caitlin	Emma, you have to go in there. You don't have a choice.
Emma	I don't want to!

Caitlin	Listen, I won't leave you alone. I won't let anything happen to you.
Emma	Promise?
Caitlin	Yeah. Now let's help Danny before he attacks Zack with the spade!

They laugh, and walk back to the boys, who have started arguing again.

Zack	Oh, just give me a go.

He pulls himself up on his one good leg and takes the spade.

Danny	Break a leg.

Zack starts jabbing the spade at the boards.

Brilliant! Just do the same thing I was doing.

Zack	*[Swinging the spade rather close to Danny's face]* SHUT UP!
Caitlin	OK, OK, I'm sure you've both loosened it up. Why don't I have a go?

Zack sulkily hands over the spade. Caitlin calmly inserts a corner of the spade between two boards and prises one off. Then another, and another. She reaches and tries the window.

Caitlin	No good: it's locked. Get back.
	Caitlin jabs the spade at the window, smashing part of it before reaching inside, unfastening and opening the window.
Danny	*[Impressed]* How hard is she!
Zack	Well if I didn't have a bad ankle…
	Emma is looking over towards the gate, across the graveyard. She takes a couple of steps away from the window. Just as she does this, the gate slams shut. They all jump.
Emma	I have a really bad feeling about this!
Zack	*[Quietly]* Yeah, it is a bit weird isn't it? Still, we have to get inside for the night.
	They all stand there looking at the window for a moment.

● ●

SCENE 2

	Inside the house (a vicarage), the window on one side of the room, an internal door on the other. **Zack, Danny, Caitlin** and **Emma** *are sitting on some chairs that have been covered with dust sheets. An old and very heavy-looking desk stands randomly in the middle of the room. Against one wall is a wooden box with Zack's backpack on the floor nearby. It is almost pitch black, except for the light from the head torches everyone other than Emma is now wearing. They sit in silence for a while.*
Danny	*[Miserably]* I'm so hungry.
Zack	Er, hello? I've broken my ankle!
	Danny groans.
Caitlin	Boys, boys!
Danny	OK, OK.
Caitlin	So, Zack, sorry about before. What were you going to say about survival situations?
Zack	Well, my dad says the first thing you have to do is…

15

Danny	Find shelter?
Zack	Well… yes, actually.
Danny	What a genius.
Zack	Shut up! We're inside now, aren't we?
Danny	Yeah, I noticed!
Emma	No thanks to you idiots. I got us here; Caitlin got us inside. All you two do is show off.
Zack	I said we're inside! That's good, right? Maybe time to stop arguing?
Danny	So now you're the boss, are you?
Caitlin	Come on, Danny.
Danny	Seriously, why's he telling us what to do?
Zack	I'm just saying there's no need to argue. We're inside, out of the rain. We can wait here until the storm blows over and we'll be fine.
Danny	Great plan. There's just one problem: these storms can last for days. What are we going to do? What's the second thing you have to do in a survival situation, Zack? Find food?
Zack	Well… yes, actually.
Danny	Hmm. There's just one problem.
Caitlin	You are good at spotting problems, Danny. Just what we all need.
Danny	We don't have any food, do we? Unless you want to go and catch us a sheep with your bare hands, Zack?
Emma	And we're in a horrible house in the middle of nowhere.
Danny	And nobody knows where we are…
Emma	And like Danny said before, these storms can last for days.
Danny	Right, so that's quite a few problems, actually. I reckon there's a good chance we'll die in here.

Caitlin	Danny! Seriously! Don't say stuff like that.
Danny	Reckon we might end up starving.
Emma	Stop it!
Danny	Although we've always got each other…
Zack	That's more like it, Danny, a bit of team spirit.
Danny	We've always got each other to eat if this goes on for too long.

Caitlin and Emma DANNY!

Danny	What? I'm being serious. Like those guys in that plane crash in South America. They survived for months eating dead bodies.
	Pause.
Zack	*[Resigned tone]* So go on then. Who would you eat, Danny?

Caitlin and Emma *[Horrified, to **Zack**]* ZACK!

Danny	Whoever died first.
Zack	Yeah, but what if you had to decide now?
Danny	Hmm. It would have to be you. Definitely. If there's one person we could do without, it would be you, Zack.
Zack	Why me?
Danny	Why not?
Zack	That's not a reason!
Emma	*[Walks over to stand next to **Zack**]* Leave him alone.
Caitlin	I'd eat Danny.
Danny	Waste of time. Not enough of me. Skin and bones, me. Has to be Zack.
Zack	I'd like to see you try!
Caitlin	Come on, why Zack?

Danny	Well, Emma found the house, so it wouldn't be fair to eat her. That just leaves you and Zack.
Caitlin	So why not me?
Danny	Seen what you did to that window. You'd kick my head in!

All laugh, then fall silent for a while.

Emma	*[Quietly]* So what are we going to do?
Danny	C'mon Zack, you're the great explorer. Let's look around and see what we can find. Unless you're needed at A&E…
Zack	Whatever! Let's go. Won't take long though, there's nothing here!

***Danny** wanders out of the room and **Zack** hobbles after him.*

Caitlin	I wonder what's in that desk.
Emma	No, don't go sniffing around, not you as well!
Caitlin	Come on, Emma, this is getting stupid.
Emma	*[Shouting]* I'm not being stupid!
Caitlin	No, I didn't mean…
Emma	I'm telling you. I've had dreams about this house. Every time I wake up really scared. There is something horrible about this place. Why can't anyone else feel it?
Caitlin	Alright. So tell me a bit more about the dreams.
Emma	Are you actually going to listen or are you going to tell me I'm crazy again?
Caitlin	Sorry, Emma. Course I'll listen.
Emma	Well, it's always the same dream. I'm outside the house. I'm looking at the window we broke in through. I can feel that someone is watching me, but I can't see anyone. I get this really scary feeling. I feel sick. I want to run away but I can't. I just stand there. And then this sound starts. It's like a scratching sound. Something scratching wood. It gets louder and louder. Someone is trying to break free of something.

	And I know that whatever it is hates me. And then I see I'm in a graveyard. And I scream. That's when I wake up.
Caitlin	That's horrible.
Emma	It's this house, Caitlin. I'm telling you. And this graveyard. Do you think there's any chance they'll find us tonight?
Caitlin	I hope so. But… I'm not saying you're making it up or anything, but we can't go out at night in the middle of nowhere in a storm. We'll end up dead. At least if we stay here you might have a scary night but you won't be in any real danger.
Emma	But what if—
Caitlin	No. You won't be in any real danger. It's not real. It's a dream. Look at me. Now say it: it's not real; it's a dream.
Emma	It's not real. It's a dream. It's not real. It's a dream.
Caitlin	OK?
Emma	OK. But don't leave me on my own, alright?
Caitlin	I won't. We'll be OK. Now come on, let's have a look in this box and see if we can find anything useful. *[She opens the box and reaches in]* Perfect! Candles. Loads of candles and candlesticks. Wow, this place must have been empty for ages. No light switches. A box full of candles. No matches though.
Emma	I bet Zack's got some. Mr Prepared. Let's have a look in his bag. Yep. Here we go.
	Emma pulls some matches out of Zack's bag and hands them to Caitlin, who lights some candles. A faint scratching noise can be heard.
Caitlin	There, that's better. Let's get a few more lit and then—
Emma	Shh! What's that noise?
Caitlin	What? Oh nothing, probably Zack.
Emma	Oh no, no; it's scratching. It's the sound from the dream…

*Emma begins to cry. **Caitlin** marches to the door and pulls it open. **Danny** and **Zack** fall through it, laughing their heads off. The scratching stops.*

Zack	Sorry, Emma!
Caitlin	You evil little… What's wrong with you two?
Zack	It was funny! *[Then, noticing **Emma** is crying]* Emma? Emma, are you OK?
Danny	Nice one, Zack.
Zack	Don't try it! It was your idea.
Danny	Emma, we're really sorry. It's going to be OK, you know. We've been right round the house and it's completely empty apart from more old furniture. There's nobody in the house, I promise.
Zack	Seriously, Emma, we didn't know you were this freaked out.
Caitlin	I can't believe you two. What were you doing listening at the door anyway? Weirdos!

Danny	Alright! We're sorry. Hey, where did you find the candles?
Emma	*[Sniffing]* In the box there.
Danny	Cool. Is there anything else in there? Let's have a look.
	Danny *reaches into the box and pulls out a large piece of paper.*
Zack	What's that?
Danny	Looks like a page from an old newspaper. Or a sort of poster.
Zack	Really old by the look of it. Has it got a date on it?
Danny	Yeah. It's a bit smudged. Looks like… Oh… It's from 1825!
Caitlin	Seriously?
Zack	Maybe that's how long it's been since someone lived here.
Danny	Could be. What's it about? Something local anyway. Can't read much of it, but the headline says 'Grave Robbed at Caldmere'.
Zack	So that's where we are! We must be in the Caldmere graveyard!
Emma	What?
Zack	Come on, have none of you heard about the Caldmere body snatcher? It's, like, the only murder story from around here. Years and years ago, the vicar was digging up the bodies in the graveyard and selling them to be dissected, or something. His daughter found out, so he killed her and her boyfriend too.
Emma	Oh no! Do you think…?
Caitlin	No! Zack, stop putting ideas in her head.
Zack	Sorry, just saying. I'm not making it up, you know.
Caitlin	Zack! Emma, it's OK.
	The scratching sound begins again, this time a lot louder.
Emma	Oh my God! What's making that noise? You said there was no one else in the house.

Caitlin	Probably... *[Hesitates]* Probably a branch on a window or something like that.
Emma	It's getting louder!
Zack	And it doesn't sound like it's coming from outside.
Danny	This is really freaky. What's going on?
Emma	I can't take this any more. Please can we get out of here? Please!

*There is a loud knock. Everyone jumps. **Emma** screams and hides behind **Caitlin**. The others freeze. There is more knocking.*

Danny	*[Whispering]* What do we do?
Zack	Shh!
Man	*[Offstage]* Hello? Is anybody there? Can I help?

*Suddenly, **Emma** runs to the broken window and leans out.*

Emma	Hello? The door's locked and we can't open it. Come round to the window. Over here.

*After some clattering around outside, a **Man** in a full-length black coat and black hat appears at the window. Throughout the rest of the play, the **Man** never looks at the person he is speaking to, except for **Emma**.*

Man	Hello. Are you OK?
Emma	Just come in—
Caitlin	What? Emma, what are you doing? We can't let some strange man—
Emma	Yes, we can. Something about this house feels wrong and I really don't fancy being stuck here on our own all night.
Danny	Alright, let's just not make a stupid decision. *[To the **Man**]* Who are you?
Man	I saw lights. This house has been empty for a long time. The weather tonight is foul. I thought you might require assistance.
Caitlin	Yes, but who are you?

22

Man	I live close by. My apologies if I frightened you, but I thought you might be experiencing some trouble. I will leave if you prefer.
Emma	No! No, please don't go.
Danny	But we don't know anything about this guy.
Emma	Yeah, well we're lost, and Zack's got a broken ankle.
Caitlin	Do you have a phone?
Man	Sadly, it has become very difficult for me to communicate with people.
Danny	No reception?
Man	Quite so. Listen, would you like me to come inside and sit with you through the storm? When it clears I can help you find your way back to your friends.
Zack	Hey! How do you know about our friends?
Man	Do you not have friends?
Zack	Well yeah, but—
Man	Good! It's settled.
Danny	No, it's not settled. We can't just let this guy in. Who knows what he wants!
Man	I understand your concern. If you ask me to leave now, I will. If you invite me in and then change your mind, I will leave as soon as you ask me to.
Emma	Couldn't we go to his house instead of this place, if he lives close by?
Caitlin	No! We're not going anywhere with this guy. But there are four of us. We should just let him in. The more people the better.
Danny	[Addressing the **Man**, reluctantly] OK, well you can come in, but you even touch one of us and we'll batter you.
Man	You are wise to be cautious child, but I simply wish to be of service.

*There is a huge clap of thunder as the **Man** climbs through the window. **Caitlin** slams it shut behind him.*

Man	Do you mind if I sit here?
Caitlin	Make yourself at home.

*The **Man** looks up sharply at this, then sits.*

Danny	Where did you say you lived?
Zack	What's your name?
Emma	You say you live near here?
Danny	Do you have a landline at your place?
Caitlin	Or any way of getting in touch with people?
Man	Unfortunately, I have been cut off for some time…
Zack	Don't suppose you've got any food, have you?
Man	My apologies, it did not occur to me…

Silence.

Emma	Do you know anything about the Caldmere body snatcher?
Caitlin	Emma, are you sure…?
Man	Child, I know rather more about the Caldmere body snatcher than anyone else you are likely to meet.
Emma	Could you tell us?
Caitlin	Emma…
Emma	I want to know. I don't just want to pretend nothing happened, or pretend that nothing is happening now.
Man	What is your name, child?
Emma	Emma Barker.
Man	*[To himself]* So it's finally happening. Here she is… *[To **Emma**]* And you want to know about the Caldmere body snatcher?

Emma	Yeah, I do.
Zack	Yeah!
Danny	Why not?
Caitlin	Hold on. I'm worried about Emma. She has bad nightmares. I don't want you making them worse.
Emma	But if I know what happened here, maybe that'll help make it all more real and less scary.
Man	Yes, it sounds to me as though the story should be told. Do you know, I have never told this story before? I know every detail, but I have never told the story. It is hard to know where to begin.
	Pause.
	Well, the story takes place nearly 200 years ago…

Act 2

●●

SCENE 1

*It is 1825. **Reverend Cameron** and **Eliza** are in the same room from the previous scene. It is light and bright and the furniture is now uncovered. The desk has been moved and now stands against the wall by the door, with some books and writing paper on it.*

Rev. Cameron	And how do your studies progress, Eliza?
Eliza	Very well, Father. Miss McCall is a good teacher.
Rev. Cameron	I have no doubt of that.

There is an awkward silence.

Eliza, on the subject of the young gentleman.

__Eliza__'s face hints at cold fury.

Eliza	*[Icily]* Samuel, Father. He has a name.
Rev. Cameron	I had hoped that we might leave all that unpleasantness in the past, Eliza.
Eliza	Really?
Rev. Cameron	Eliza, I know that you feel anger, perhaps even hatred towards me. But please believe that I acted out of love for you.
Eliza	Not out of a father's jealousy? You came between us… *[She chokes on the words]* You forbade me to see Samuel because you want me to be your little child forever. I am not a child any more. You are trying to protect something that only exists in the past.
Rev. Cameron	NO! I am trying to protect your future, Eliza. Not what you were, but what you could be. Eliza, you were not born to be a carpenter's wife!

Eliza	And why not? Jesus was a carpenter. You have spent your whole life in service to a one-thousand-eight-hundred-and-twenty-five-year-old carpenter. Why should I not marry a living one?
Rev. Cameron	You test my patience, girl. I have forbidden you to see the boy and that is my final word. You have many advantages in this life, Eliza. Do not throw them all away for a love that will pass. In years to come you will look back at this and chide yourself for doubting your father's wisdom. You will not marry him. You will not see him. Not my daughter!
Eliza	You have no right—
Rev. Cameron	I have every right! I am your father! You will do as I say or you will leave this house, forever!
Eliza	You will not have this power over me for long, Father.
Rev. Cameron	*[In a softer voice]* And it is better for you that for now I do. Eliza, I am doing this for you, not for me. Think on that.
Eliza	Be warned, Father, you may come to regret this... If Mother were still alive—
Rev. Cameron	How dare you!
	*Eliza storms out of the room and slams the door. **Reverend Cameron** wanders over to the desk and taps at it, muttering to himself in agitation. **Mrs Barker**, the housekeeper, enters.*
Mrs Barker	Excuse me, sir, I shall come back later.
Rev. Cameron	No, no, Mrs Barker. Carry on.
	***Mrs Barker** begins moving silently round the room, dusting. Both are silent for a while.*
	She is too young! How can she know what is right for her life when she has lived so little of it?
	***Mrs Barker** stops dusting. She seems unsure whether she is expected to respond.*

	Am I not her father?
Mrs Barker	Well, sir, she is sixteen years old. Young ladies are known to lose their tempers.
Rev. Cameron	With her it is more than an issue of temper, as you know. She is not ready for the world. Ever since her mother died she has seemed to be leaning over a precipice towards madness. She is not ready to be courting.
Mrs Barker	*[Quietly]* Yes indeed, sir, I have witnessed her outbursts. So have my children…
Rev. Cameron	My apologies for Eliza's outbursts towards your daughters will never be sufficient.
Mrs Barker	There is no need. Maybe when Eliza is older she will understand that you are simply a loving father, sir.
Rev. Cameron	I pray daily that the Lord makes her path a little brighter.
Mrs Barker	Yes, sir.
Rev. Cameron	Thank you, Mrs Barker, I shall leave you to your work.

*He walks out of the room. A few moments pass. **Mrs Barker** walks to the door and calls through it.*

Mrs Barker	Children? Girls?

*After a few moments Mrs Barker's daughters, **Bess** and **Nelly**, come running into the room.*

	Girls, I have a job for you. One which you'll be good at, I'll bet!
Bess	What is it, Ma?
Mrs Barker	It's Mistress Eliza. I worry about her.
Nelly	Is she ill, Ma? Ha! Serves her right. Only yesterday she slapped me just for looking at her, the witch!
Mrs Barker	You watch your tongue! No, I don't have reason to think that she is ill, not in the way you mean, anyway. I want you to keep an eye on her for me. Just come back and tell me if she

starts doing anything strange. She's not been herself lately and we don't want her doing any damage. To herself, her father or anyone else!

Bess   You want us to spy on her, Ma? What if we get caught?

Mrs Barker   Don't get caught. You've got a knack for that, haven't you?

Nelly   OK, Ma. Anything strange and we'll tell you.

Mrs Barker   That's my girls.

She bustles off out of the room.

Bess   How exciting!

Nelly   I wonder why Ma's so concerned about Mistress Eliza. She hates us and we've never done her wrong.

Bess   Something's wrong with her, alright. We might find out what it is if we keep watching.

Nelly   We might be able to pay her back for all them slaps too…

They walk out of the room together.

● ●

SCENE 2

The graveyard at night. **Eliza** *enters from the vicarage, walks to the middle of the graveyard and paces back and forth. The* **Barker girls** *creep out after her and hide behind two gravestones.*

Eliza   What to do, what to do! Where is Samuel? Why does it have to be this way? Father is a beast. A BEAST! Why is he doing this to me? Where is Samuel? Oh my soul, I will have to leave now. I will not stay in this house. I will not stop myself from seeing Samuel. If Father finds us out again, who knows what might happen? No, no, far better just to leave. Oh, I love him so much! Here he is. Is that him? *[She walks to the gate and calls quietly]* Samuel? Samuel? Is that you? *[Then, as* **Samuel** *enters, out of breath]* Oh, it's so good to see you! I thought you wouldn't come. But here you are. Good, good, I have much to tell you.

Samuel	Heavens! Give me a moment to catch my breath, would you? And you'd better lower your voice. We have to be careful. A lot of people in the village respect your father, and I don't want to be more on his wrong side than I have to be. *[Scratches his behind, sits down and sighs]* Phew!
Eliza	Are you happy to see me?
Samuel	Course I am.
Eliza	Well, you don't seem it! Here I am, fretting and worrying about when you'll arrive, and you just moan and scratch your—
Samuel	Ah, OK, OK! Of course I'm happy to see you. Give me a kiss and stop your fretting.
	Eliza turns away. Samuel rolls his eyes.
Samuel	So, what's the matter now then, eh?
Eliza	It's my father.

Samuel	You haven't been speaking to him about us any further, have you?
Eliza	I couldn't help it. He mentioned the subject.
Samuel	I told you to keep your secrets!
Eliza	I know. I thought maybe I might change his mind, but it's no use. He's set against you and that's not going to change. He thinks I should wait for a scholar, or a doctor, or someone of some sort of learning.
Samuel	Aye, carpentry's just for fools, eh?
Eliza	Oh come on, it's not what I think.
Samuel	Well, nothing has changed then; we'll just have to keep things to ourselves.
Eliza	Yes, but what about the future, Samuel?
Samuel	The future?
Eliza	The future. We can't keep our love secret forever.
Samuel	Can't we?
Eliza	NO!
Samuel	Shh!
Eliza	No. We're in love, we want to spend our lives together. How can we do that if we pretend it's not happening?
Samuel	Well...
Eliza	*[Icily]* Samuel, do you love me or do you not?
Samuel	Well...
Eliza	Because if you do not love me then leave now and do not come back.
Samuel	Eliza...
Eliza	But if you do love me as I love you then we will spend our lives together, won't we?

Samuel	Well…
Eliza	Won't we?
Samuel	*[Uncertainly]* Well, yes, of course.
Eliza	Are you sure about that?
Samuel	*[Hastily]* Very sure!
Eliza	Then there's only one way we can carry on, can't you see?
Samuel	And what's that then, girl?
Eliza	We need to get married.
Samuel	WHAT?
Eliza	Shh!
Samuel	Married?
Eliza	We need to get married. Once we're married, he'll have to accept us. He'll have no choice.
Samuel	But Eliza, he will disown you if we continue.
Eliza	Well, at least this way we'll be together.
Samuel	But… but Eliza, I don't have a house, I live with my father.
Eliza	We'll run away!
Samuel	WHAT?
Eliza	Shh!
Samuel	Run away?
Eliza	We'll run away and get married, Samuel. The romance! Think of it.
Samuel	Yes, I am thinking of it. Now I love you, Eliza, but this is madness. I don't have any money and nor do you.
Eliza	Yes, I thought you might worry about money. But, the thing is, I do have money, Samuel.
Samuel	You mean your father has money!

Eliza	No, I have my own money, and more coming. By this time tomorrow I will have fifty pounds.
Samuel	Eliza, how have you possibly come to have that much money?
Eliza	It doesn't matter. We can afford to run away. We can be together. That's all that matters now. We can run away to Edinburgh. And we can get married. And you can set up shop as a carpenter. And we can have babies—
Samuel	WHAT?
Eliza	Shh!
Samuel	Sorry. Babies?
Eliza	Samuel, we're getting married, of course there will be babies. Has nobody ever told you how that happens? You should ask—
Samuel	Don't be stupid, girl. I know how babies happen. I just hadn't planned on having any of my own too soon, that's all.
Eliza	Oh, but think how happy we'll be, Samuel! You, me, the children, the city. Samuel, go back home and prepare yourself for our new life together. Meet me back here tomorrow night and we can make our plans for leaving.
Samuel	Eliza, what are you talking about? We are not running away!
Eliza	[Staring hard at **Samuel**] What? Don't you want to be with me?
Samuel	[Hesitantly] Of course I do, yes, yes. OK, I'll come tomorrow and maybe you will have calmed down.
Eliza	Oh, Samuel, I love you so much!
Samuel	Er… I love you too, girl.
Eliza	Now you'd better be leaving before I'm missed. And Samuel?
Samuel	Yes.

Eliza	Tomorrow, come an hour after midnight.
Samuel	So late?
Eliza	Yes, we won't be fin… I just won't be able to get out before then.
Samuel	Tomorrow then. An hour after midnight.
Eliza	Goodbye, Samuel.
Samuel	Goodbye, sweetheart.

*They embrace, before **Samuel** exits the graveyard through the gate.*

Eliza	*[Triumphantly]* Hah! Father, you will hold me no more! Within a week I'll be gone forever and it will be your doing.

***Eliza** wanders happily back into the vicarage. The **Barker girls** stand up behind their gravestones.*

Nelly	What are we going to do?
Bess	Ma's fears can't have been this bad.
Nelly	Bad?
Bess	Well, she's talking about going against her father, running off with Samuel, leaving the house and never coming back! If we tell her father, he will get himself into a rage. Imagine the fight they'll have, the two of them. I hope we can be there to see it!
Nelly	Sister, do you like Mistress Eliza?
Bess	Of course not, that's why I hope we can see what her father does to her!
Nelly	Well, there is something else. Neither of us likes her.
Bess	No.
Nelly	And she don't like us, neither.
Bess	True.
Nelly	And she's talking about leaving forever and never coming back.

Bess	Yes… OOOOH we don't have to tell anyone! Then she'd go and we'd all be happy. Except—
Nelly	What?
Bess	Well, except Reverend Cameron. Mistress Eliza may be mean, but she is his daughter. And he lost his wife. Imagine how he must want to keep Eliza close to him. We have to tell him.

● ●

SCENE 3

*In the vicarage, **Mrs Barker** is cleaning. **Reverend Cameron** enters, carrying a book which he places absent-mindedly on the desk.*

Rev. Cameron	Mrs Barker, tell me, have you heard any talk lately of the terrible ghouls who robbed poor Mrs McArdle's grave and took her body?
Mrs Barker	No, sir. But at least we haven't had any more trouble like that.
Rev. Cameron	Well no, not here at Caldmere. It was a bad business when it happened, though. It's happening all over the country. It beggars belief that people are willing to dig up the corpses of fellow human beings and sell them. And the anatomy schools who buy them are no better. They know where the bodies come from. They ask no questions, I'll warrant.
Mrs Barker	A terrible sin, sir.
Rev. Cameron	Yes. But you have heard no speculation in the village about this horrid practice returning to Caldmere?
Mrs Barker	None, sir.
Rev. Cameron	It just seems strange to me that it should only have happened once. These fiends make a business of taking bodies. We've had ten or so burials these six months since Mrs McArdle's. They could have made a lot of money out of us, I expect. We buried old Tom Hutchinson only three days ago.

Mrs Barker	Well, sir, if I may be so bold, perhaps we should just be thankful that they have not returned.
Rev. Cameron	Quite right, Mrs Barker; quite right. No sense in dwelling on something so repugnant. I shall be off. Good day, Mrs Barker.
Mrs Barker	Good day, sir.

Reverend Cameron leaves the room. His book remains on the desk. Mrs Barker continues to clean. In walk the Barker girls.

| Mrs Barker | Good morning, my dears. |
| Nelly and Bess | Morning, Ma! |

The Barker girls walk to the other end of the room and have a hushed conversation.

Nelly	Are you sure we should tell?
Bess	We agreed.
Nelly	But we don't know what will happen.
Bess	We're just telling Ma, though. It's up to her whether we tell anyone else.

Nelly nods. They wander over to the middle of the room.

Nelly	Ma, it's about Mistress Eliza.
Mrs Barker	Yes, dear?
Nelly	Well, you asked us to keep an eye on her...

Mrs Barker puts down her duster and turns around warily.

Bess	Well we just did as you asked, Ma.
Mrs Barker	You weren't seen, were you?
Nelly	No, Ma, don't worry, but we did see something.
Mrs Barker	Go on.

Reverend Cameron re-enters the room to pick up the book he left. He is not seen by the Barkers.

Nelly	Ma, Mistress Eliza has some awful plans.
	Reverend Cameron freezes.
Bess	We saw her going out late last night.
Nelly	So we followed her out into the graveyard.
Bess	We hid behind a gravestone so she couldn't see.
Nelly	And up came Samuel Miller. They're still courting in secret!
Mrs Barker	Oh dear, I feared as much!
Bess	It gets worse, Ma. She's got some money.
Nelly	And they're planning to get married.
Mrs Barker	WHAT?
Nelly	Shh!
Mrs Barker	Married!
Bess	And first they're going to run away to Edinburgh!
Nelly	And she says they'll never see Reverend Cameron again.
Mrs Barker	Oh dear, the poor man! That girl will destroy him!
Bess	But, Ma, if we tell him, who knows what he will do to her?
Rev. Cameron	I am not a monster, child.
	The Barkers spin round.
Mrs Barker	*[Breathlessly]* Oh Reverend Cameron, sir, I didn't see you there.
Rev. Cameron	No.
Mrs Barker	Did you hear what the children said, sir?
Rev. Cameron	Every word, Mrs Barker. Now children, you must answer me truthfully. Have you exaggerated the facts at all? Have you in any way altered what was said between them?
Nelly	No, sir.
Rev. Cameron	Then they really do plan to leave Caldmere?

Nelly	I think so, sir.
Bess	Sir, there is one thing.
Rev. Cameron	Yes, child?
Bess	Sir, it seemed to me that the lady was more keen on the plan than Mr Miller, sir.
Rev. Cameron	You mean he may not wish to leave?
Bess	I don't know, sir. The plan was Mistress Eliza's though.
Rev. Cameron	I owe you my thanks.
Mrs Barker	Go on now, girls. Let's give Reverend Cameron some peace. You go on and play.
Rev. Cameron	Just one more thing, please.
Nelly and Bess	Yes, sir?
Rev. Cameron	Children, I would rather you stopped watching Mistress Eliza.

*The **Barker girls** leave the room.*

Rev. Cameron	Mrs Barker, a few words, if you don't mind.
Mrs Barker	Sir, I do hope I haven't caused any trouble.
Rev. Cameron	No, no, you have done very well. I know you acted out of loyalty to me and I thank you for it. Mrs Barker, I am going to investigate this matter myself. I would be grateful if you and your children would keep out of the way. I do not wish to be watched. I do not wish for this business to be public. I have some pride. Is that understood?
Mrs Barker	Quite understood. Sir, would you like me to speak to Samuel Miller for you? I know his mother. A good family, sir.
Rev. Cameron	Absolutely not, Mrs Barker. I wish to deal with this whole affair in my own way. Have I made myself clear?
Mrs Barker	Oh, perfectly clear, sir. I shall say nothing.
Rev. Cameron	Your tact at this painful time is much appreciated, Mrs Barker. Good day.

Mrs Barker   Good day, sir.

● ●

SCENE 4

The graveyard at night. There are two young men onstage, dressed all in black. **Macfarlane** *is up to his chest in a hole he is digging near a gravestone. He passes a bag of earth up to* **Fettes**, *who is standing next to the hole. A lantern rests on top of the gravestone.*

Macfarlane   Where are you, Tom Hutchinson? Rouse yourself!

Fettes   Are you utterly determined to condemn us both to hell, Macfarlane? These jests! You are tunnelling into the man's grave! Stop it!

Macfarlane   Yes, good idea, I need a rest. This gets harder every time we do it! I still think we should just stick to digging up the graves directly. Much easier.

Fettes	Yes, Macfarlane, but we'd be caught, just as we were nearly caught after taking Mrs McArdle. This is much safer. We dig down a short distance away from the grave and then tunnel across. Nobody suspects a thing.
Macfarlane	Nobody?
Fettes	Nobody.
Macfarlane	No body? Eh? No body? *[Fettes just glares at him]* Still, all in an honourable cause, eh Fettes?
Fettes	You call this honourable? Resurrecting corpses from their graves by night? *[Shakes his head]* Carrying them off to be cut into pieces on a slab?
Macfarlane	We have been through this argument so many times. By doing this we are helping Dr K. teach us how the body works. All so we can save lives.
Fettes	It still can't be right. Look around at these graves. Here lies Arthur Coates. No, he doesn't. He had a big heart which we cut out. Here lies Laura McArdle. No, she doesn't. But what an interesting brain she had. How long can this go on?
Macfarlane	As long as we need bodies. As long as the country needs surgeons. As long as surgeons need training. And for as long as the law limits the study of human anatomy to the bodies of executed criminals. Come on, why so grave tonight?
Fettes	Macfarlane, show some respect for this place!
Macfarlane	Boy, we are about to remove the body of Tom Hutchinson from his grave, three days after he was buried. No amount of respect is going to make up for that if your conscience is getting the better of you. Here, have a drink. *[Hands over a hip flask, from which **Fettes** takes a long swig]* Now, let's get back to it. In fact, why don't you get down here and do some digging?
	They swap places.
Fettes	What about the girl? Should we wait for her?

Macfarlane	She told us where to look. She'll be out soon enough for her money. Quite a little fortune she must be building up. I wonder what she's planning.
	Fettes picks up the spade and begins digging. They work without speaking for a short while, Fettes occasionally stopping to pass a sackful of earth up to Macfarlane. Eliza enters from the vicarage and walks over towards the grave. She is followed silently by Reverend Cameron, who stands unseen in the shadows and watches the scene unfold.
Eliza	Mr Macfarlane? Mr Macfarlane? Mr Fettes? Oh, I see work is well underway. Good. Poor old Tom. Still, he has no need for his body any more.
Macfarlane	Just as I was trying to say to Mr Fettes, madam.
Eliza	Are you nearly finished, gentlemen?
Macfarlane	Indeed we are, madam. Not long now and we will have Mr Hutchinson up and about.
Fettes	*[Sharply]* Macfarlane!
	Fettes passes up a bag of earth which Macfarlane hoists out.
Eliza	Would you care to give me the money you owe now?
Macfarlane	I would sooner wait until we have the body, madam.
Eliza	That's fair.
Fettes	Macfarlane, pay attention!
	Macfarlane hoists out another bag of earth.
Eliza	Mr Macfarlane?
Macfarlane	Yes, madam?
Eliza	This is a sordid business.
Macfarlane	Yes, I dare say it is.
Eliza	But I have enjoyed it.
Macfarlane	How do you mean?

Eliza	Well, it is unusual for a young lady of my upbringing to make any money, really, whether inside the law or outside it.
Macfarlane	And it is unusual for a young lady of any upbringing to sell corpses in a graveyard, madam.
Fettes	Macfarlane, for heaven's sake, this is a job for two!

Macfarlane hoists out another bag of earth.

Eliza	Yes, quite. And I have enjoyed that.
Macfarlane	Do you mean that it is to stop?
Eliza	I do. You may do as you wish, of course. I won't try to stop you continuing to visit this graveyard after burials. But this will be my last body. I will be leaving soon.
Macfarlane	Marriage?
Eliza	Yes, marriage.
Macfarlane	Well I hope the young gentleman is of a similarly... adventurous nature.
Eliza	Oh yes, he is.
Fettes	Macfarlane!
Macfarlane	Yes, Fettes, be calm and keep your voice low!
Fettes	I have the body. Are you ready?
Macfarlane	As ever.

*There are pushing and shoving and grunting noises from **Fettes,** who eventually stands up in the grave with his arms around a corpse rolled up in muddy sacking.*

Here he is.

*Macfarlane takes hold of the body and hoists it out of the grave. As he does so he trips backwards and the corpse falls into Eliza. The canvas drops away from the top end of the corpse, revealing the wide-eyed and grinning face of the dead Tom Hutchinson. **Eliza** screams.*

Macfarlane	Madam, silence! Please accept my apologies, but be quiet! We are all finished if your father hears us.
Eliza	His face! He was staring at me! He knew me!
Macfarlane	He was dead, madam.
	She shudders violently.
Eliza	I am glad to be out of this business. Grinning! As if he would have the last laugh…
	Fettes *is struggling to get out of the grave.*
Fettes	Macfarlane? Macfarlane!
	Macfarlane *absent-mindedly offers his hand to* ***Fettes*** *who climbs out of the grave, pulls the spade out and leans it against the gravestone.*
Macfarlane	Madam, it was nothing. Take your money and may you enjoy good fortune in your new life.
	Shaking, she takes the money he offers.
Fettes	Good night, madam.

Macfarlane	And good luck.

Fettes and Macfarlane take the body between them, and exit through the gate, leaving the spade behind. Eliza stays where she is, staring down at the grave.

Eliza	He knew. He knew what I was doing. I know it. That grin!
Rev. Cameron	Does your conscience trouble you, Eliza?

She screams again and turns round.

Eliza	*[Shocked and guilty]* Oh dear heaven! It's you, Father!
Rev. Cameron	How many bodies, Eliza?
Eliza	*[Defiantly]* Ten. How did you know?

Reverend Cameron advances towards Eliza, never taking his eyes from hers.

Rev. Cameron	*[Shaking with anger]* Mrs Barker's children told me of your plans with Samuel, but that is not important. What have you become, Eliza? I was so proud of you. So was your mother. Did we fail you so badly? We loved you, educated you, protected you. And this is how you repay us? You steal bodies from graves? In our own graveyard? Bodies that I myself have buried. Souls that I have prayed for!
Eliza	I did not choose this, Father. You tried to take Samuel from me. He is the only thing in this life that I care about. And I will not let him go. I did what I had to. I needed money to escape this place. I am leaving, Father. If you wish to stop me, you will have to kill me.
Rev. Cameron	Child, child! I did what I thought was best for you, as any father would. I know you could not understand that, but to desecrate graves! That is no way to build a future. How will you live? How will you sleep? You have sinned terribly. What have you done?
Eliza	I have done what I had to do. That is all.
Rev. Cameron	Go then! Go! Live your life, if you can. I am going to find Constable Stevenson. Do not be here when I return with

him. If this is freedom, you are free. I thank the Lord that your mother did not live to see this, Eliza. She would have disowned you.

Reverend Cameron rushes off through the gate. Eliza stands by the grave, rocking slightly.

Eliza   Father? Papa? *[She shivers and wraps her arms around herself.]* Mama, Mama.

Samuel enters through the gate.

Samuel   Eliza? Here I am! An hour after midnight on the pin! But I was nearly spotted by your father! He was flying down the hill so fast he nearly ran straight into me. I just had time to jump behind a tree. Not that he would have noticed me, I'll bet. He was in a fury! What was he doing? *[Then, noticing Eliza's numb state]* Eliza? Are you ill, girl? What has happened?

He reaches out and touches her shoulder. She jumps and notices him for the first time.

Eliza   Oh, Samuel.

She collapses into his arms, sobbing.

Samuel   What is it, Eliza? What happened?

Eliza   *[Pouring out the words]* My life here is over. My mother is dead and my father wants me dead. The Constable is coming. Oh, what a price! What a price for love! *[She pauses and takes a few deep breaths, composing herself]* But I do love you, Samuel, I do love you. We must leave now. Come with me, I'll fetch some food and clothes from the house. We must leave tonight.

Samuel   Eliza, I am not ready.

Eliza   We have no choice; in a matter of hours the Constable will be here for me. We must leave.

Samuel   The Constable? Why will he be coming for you?

Eliza   Oh Samuel, don't ask, don't ask. Just say we can leave now.

Samuel	Eliza, I came to tell you I can't leave Caldmere. I just can't leave. This is where I belong. You, too.

Eliza pulls away and stands very still, looking at the ground.

Eliza	You mean, you will not leave with me?
Samuel	No, Eliza, stay. Let's both stay and we can find a way. We are still young. Maybe your father will change his mind when you are a little older. We do not have to do everything this instant.
Eliza	But I have risked so much.
Samuel	What have you risked?
Eliza	I have done so much, and you have done nothing. I have put our love above all else, and you… you have treated it like a passing fancy.
Samuel	Eliza, why do you believe we have to leave? Why has your father gone for the Constable? *[He notices the hole in the ground and the spade]* Eliza, is this a new grave?
Eliza	*[Very quietly]* Samuel, I love you. My father will not let us be together, but I do not accept his will. We will be together. I have done what I can to make it possible for us to escape. I have done everything I can. I have made such sacrifices for us. I have worked harder than you can imagine to find the money we need to escape. Do not tell me that we cannot leave, Samuel. It will kill me.
Samuel	Eliza, what do you mean? What have you done for money?

She points at the hole in the ground.

Eliza	What do you imagine?
Samuel	What? No, not this! Eliza, are you mad? What were you thinking? Stealing corpses? And do you think I want to build a life on this? You think this is love?
Eliza	No, Samuel, please. Please. This could still end happily. Come with me. Be my love forever. Leave with me tonight.

Samuel   You are mad. You are truly mad!

Eliza   Mad with love for you.

Samuel   How can you say that and do this?

Eliza stoops and picks up the spade.

Eliza   Then you are abandoning me also? You, who I risked
everything for. You, who I would have followed to the end of
the world. You are abandoning me. Like my mother. Like my
father. You will not leave here without me. YOU WILL NOT
LEAVE HERE!

*As she shouts this, she pulls the spade up and swings it viciously
at Samuel's head. He cries out and falls to the floor, motionless.
Eliza stands over him for a moment, the spade held high as if to
bring it down again on his head. She falters and drops it.*

Samuel? Samuel? Oh no, no, no! My poor love! Samuel?
Samuel? So much blood!

*She sits down and cradles him in her arms, stroking his head.
His eyes are open and his face is covered in blood.*

What have I done? What have I done?

*She gets to her feet and starts pacing frantically around. She stumbles into **Samuel**'s body and looks down, horrified all over again.*

Samuel, why have you done this to us? Why is this happening? We could have been happy! But now we are damned. Damned! You are to blame and you are punished. But I could have forgiven you. My father is to blame. I will never forgive him. And the Barker children. I will have my revenge. I will not rest! I will not rest...

*She bends down, reaches under **Samuel**'s arms, drags him and drops him into the open grave. She looks around again, then runs off through the gate.*

• •

SCENE 5

*The vicarage, the next morning. Looking pale, dirty and haggard, **Eliza** enters and creeps silently across the floor. She stops in the middle of the room and kneels down. She pulls up a floorboard and reaches into the floor, pulling out a bag of coins. As she replaces the floorboard, there is a loud and urgent knocking at the door. **Mrs Barker** can be heard answering the front door to **Constable Stevenson**. **Eliza** freezes, and listens to the conversation happening offstage.*

Stevenson	Open up, open up!
Mrs Barker	Oh, good morning to you, Constable. Did I keep you waiting? I am sorry. Do come in. Reverend Cameron? Reverend Cameron, sir? Oh dear me, where is he?
Stevenson	Mrs Barker, it is my unpleasant duty to inform you that Reverend Cameron is under arrest.
Mrs Barker	There must be some mistake. Reverend Cameron under arrest? Have you gone mad, Constable?
Stevenson	He spent the night under lock and key, Mrs Barker. I can assure you I am not mad.
Mrs Barker	But what do you think he has done? Whatever it is you are wrong, of course!

Stevenson	It is very hard to believe, I admit. He came to me, Mrs Barker, and confessed that he had been responsible for stealing Mrs McArdle's body from her grave.

*With each development concerning her father, **Eliza**'s face contorts with delight.*

Eliza	The old fool, I will see they hang him!
Mrs Barker	Now look here, Constable—
Stevenson	Mrs Barker, you must let Wallace and me in. We will need to search the house for evidence of any further crimes. A man capable of the things Reverend Cameron has admitted to may be capable of anything. To betray the community like this. A wretched, evil, cruel man! Now let me in!

*__Eliza__ looks around frantically for a hiding place. Seeing none that will do, she quickly pulls up the floorboard again, and another next to it. She slips into the floor, pulling the boards back into place on top of her, just as **Constable Stevenson** and **Constable Wallace** enter the room.*

Stevenson	Right then, Wallace, I will need to speak with each of the residents. Bring that desk over here to the middle of the room. And two chairs.
	Constable Wallace drags the desk across the floor and places it directly over Eliza's hiding place, where it was in Act 1. He then places two chairs on opposite sides of the desk. Constable Stevenson sits down and puts on some spectacles.
Stevenson	Search the house and grounds, Wallace. [Constable Wallace *walks out and can be heard banging around*] Is there anyone else in the house, Mrs Barker?
Mrs Barker	My children, Constable, and Mistress Eliza.
Stevenson	Please would you call them in?
Mrs Barker	They're not in any trouble are they?
Stevenson	I very much doubt it, Mrs Barker, but I need to talk to them, and to you. Now please, I know this has come as a shock, but try to pull yourself together.
Mrs Barker	Oh, yes, Constable.
Stevenson	The children, Mrs Barker? And Eliza? And if you wouldn't mind, I would rather not tell them why I am here to begin with.
Mrs Barker	Oh dear!
	She goes to the door and calls out.
	Children? CHILDREN! Come to the parlour please, children. Constable Stevenson needs to talk to us.
	They wait in silence until the Barker girls enter, looking confused by Constable Stevenson's presence.
Mrs Barker	Say good mornin' to the Constable, children.
Bess and Nelly	Good mornin', Constable Stevenson.
Mrs Barker	Bess, would you go and find Mistress Eliza? The Constable needs to speak to her also.

Bess exits. There is a nervous silence.

Constable, you are making a mistake, I tell you. Only yesterday he was saying how he couldn't understand why anyone would rob graves. He wouldn't do it. Not Reverend Cameron. He just wouldn't.

Stevenson He has confessed to it, Mrs Barker. He also confessed to stealing the bodies of nine other poor souls since Mrs McArdle. Apparently he sold them to a couple of young doctors for dissection, but he refuses to provide any more detail than that.

*There is a shout from **Constable Wallace** and a scream from **Bess**. They run onstage.*

Wallace [*Panting*] He was in an open grave outside. It's Samuel Miller, sir. Blood all over his head. Murder, no doubt about it.

Stevenson A murder! Bess, have you found Mistress Eliza?

Bess No, sir, she is nowhere in the house.

Mrs Barker And I didn't hear her rise this morning. Oh my, you don't think…?

Stevenson Think what, Mrs Barker?

Mrs Barker You don't think she's been killed, do you?

Stevenson Is there some reason that you think that, Mrs Barker?

Mrs Barker Well, Mistress Eliza and Samuel Miller… oh dear! They were in love, you see. And Reverend Cameron was against it. He told her she was forbidden to see him, but she was of an age when girls don't take kindly to being forbidden to do anything. And the children here overheard Mistress Eliza and Samuel making a plan to elope. And Reverend Cameron got to hear of it, even though I didn't mean for him to hear. Oh dear, this is all my fault!

She begins sobbing.

Stevenson Mrs Barker, please. Are you saying that Samuel Miller was visiting Eliza in secret?

Mrs Barker	*[Between sobs]* Yes.
Stevenson	And he visited last night?
Mrs Barker	Yes.
Stevenson	And did Reverend Cameron know the lad was coming?
Mrs Barker	Oh... yes, he knew.
Stevenson	Then I am afraid the future is looking bleak for Reverend Cameron, Mrs Barker. Bleak and short.
Mrs Barker	Oh, my dears!

She hugs the children, still sobbing.

Stevenson	Mrs Barker, may I suggest that you accompany me into the village with the children? You can stay with one of the families there, I am sure. You will not want to remain here, I imagine? We can collect your belongings at another time. I will attempt to persuade Reverend Cameron to tell me where Eliza is. And if he will not tell me, we will form a search party with the villagers.
Mrs Barker	Right you are, sir. Come on, children. We'll go with Constable Stevenson, shall we? Come on now.

She ushers them out of the room, and out of the vicarage.
Constable Stevenson *stands up and looks around the room.*
He speaks thoughtfully to himself.

Stevenson	Eliza, wherever you are, I hope you are alive. But alive or dead, you must have left a trace... You must have left a trace.

*He turns and walks out of the room, shutting the door behind him. He and **Constable Wallace** and **the Barkers** can be heard making their way away from the vicarage. When the sound of their departure has faded to nothing, we hear a knocking sound. **Eliza** is trying to get out from under the floorboards, but the desk is too heavy and the floorboards will not move. The knocking becomes more and more frantic. Soon it is interspersed with scratching, and muffled cries for help. The scratching sounds build to a crescendo and then stop abruptly.*

Act 3

SCENE 1

> *The graveyard, back in the present day.* **Zack, Danny, Caitlin, Emma** *and the* **Man** *have moved outside. The storm has died down but it is still dark. The* **Man** *continues to avoid looking at the person he is speaking to, unless it is* **Emma**.

Man   As I have said, if you don't believe me then look around at the gravestones.

> *He leads them from one to the next,* **Zack** *hobbling painfully. The person who reads out the epitaph stays by that gravestone.*

Man   Here lies Tom Hutchinson, 1762–1825.

Zack   Laura McArdle, 1771–1825.

Danny   Samuel Miller, 1808–1825.

Caitlin	Arthur Coates, 1783–1825.
Emma	*[Standing in the centre stage]* Barker. The girls were called Barker. That's my name. And the nightmares…
Danny	Oh, come on! He lives nearby. He asked you what your name was. He knows the names on the gravestones and he made a story up.
Zack	But the Caldmere body snatcher was real.
Danny	Yeah, well he's taken the story and made something out of it. Look, old guy, it was a good story but it doesn't make sense.
Man	It is a true story. The mysteries of the soul do not always appear to be bound by logic.
Danny	Whatever. Here's why it doesn't make sense. If you were Eliza, and you needed some money, why dig up bodies? There must have been other ways to make money!
Man	It was not so easy at that time, especially for a young woman. And she needed the money fast. She could never have found fifty pounds legally.
Caitlin	Well, here's another thing. So, it was really hard to get hold of that kind of money, but she had managed it. And it was in the house under the floorboards. And she wanted to escape after killing Samuel. So why did she leave it until the next morning to go and get the money?
Man	*[Very sadly]* Because in one moment of passion she had just killed the man she loved. Her heart was broken. Who can say that their mind would be clear in those circumstances?
Emma	*[Quietly]* What happened to her anyway?
Man	*[Turning away]* I do not wish to speak of it.
Zack	Oh come on, you can't leave that bit out! Was she rescued?
Man	*[Sighs deeply]* She died under the floorboards.
Zack	That's just sick. A body snatcher who buried herself alive by accident!

Caitlin	Shut up, Zack.
Danny	So what about Reverend Cameron? What happened to him?
Man	He was tried for the murders of Samuel and Eliza.
Zack	What? No way! How come they didn't figure it out?
Man	As he ran down to find the Constable that night, he had a change of heart. He had meant to tell the truth. That Eliza had been disinterring the bodies to sell them. He believed that the families should know. He had hoped that Eliza would run away and never be caught, but the further he ran, the less sure he became. How could he accuse his own daughter? What if she were caught? No, he decided that he must take the blame for the crimes. It would mean disgrace and punishment, but it was better for him to suffer than for his daughter. So, he found the Constable and confessed. Little did he know that, as he did so, Eliza was murdering Samuel.
Zack	But what about when the Constable accused him of Samuel's murder?
Man	When that happened, Reverend Cameron's heart finally broke. He knew that it must have been Eliza who murdered Samuel, and he knew he was partly to blame for all these events. He should have seen that she needed Samuel and not forbidden them to meet. He was wracked with guilt. When it became clear that the police thought he had murdered Eliza too, he saw one final chance to protect her. He thought she must have run away. He would say nothing. He would let them believe he had killed her also. He would be tried and executed, and she would be free. So he thought.
Danny	I still don't believe it.
Zack	It doesn't matter whether we believe it or not. It's a good story anyway!
Emma	*[Nervously]* I have a question. Eliza killed Samuel. She swore she would make her father pay and she did that, alright. And she swore she would find a way to make the Barker children pay. What about that bit? Did they pay?

Man	Not in a way that I am aware of, child, no. Not yet, at least.
Caitlin	Not yet? What do you mean by that?
Man	*[To Emma]* It has not escaped your attention that you share the same surname as the children who spied on Eliza all those years ago.
Danny	*[Sarcastically]* Yes, what a coincidence!
Man	*[To Emma]* It is up to you what you believe. You have been having strange nightmares recently?
Caitlin	Oh come on, that's not fair! You know she has.
Man	And has anything of my story resonated with those dreams, child?
Caitlin	Hey, stop it! Leave her alone!
Man	This is important! The dreams, Emma. Have they been about this place? Have they been about Eliza?
Emma	*[Looking to Caitlin]* I'm scared.
Caitlin	Right, that's it. You are going to have to leave. You're messing with our heads. This isn't right.
Man	Listen to me. You must see what is happening. This house is haunted by the ghost of Eliza Cameron, and, mark my words, hers is a vengeful, evil ghost. If you have been drawn here by her, then you are in danger. You would do well to keep me here, or else leave with me.
Danny	She said go. Go on, leave us alone!
	***Danny** makes to grab the **Man**, but he steps calmly and easily out of the way.*
Man	Do not dismiss my warning. You are in danger. That is why I came. The young are at greatest risk around her. Adults do not seem to see ghosts. But you… Do not go back into the house. You must leave with me now.
Danny	No chance, mate. *[Holds the spade back ready to swing]* I said go!

	*The **Man** does not move. **Danny** swings and the **Man** sways out of the way again.*
Man	You should believe me. Has it not occurred to you to ask how I came to know so much?
	He unbuttons his coat and it falls to the floor. He takes off his hat. He is wearing the clothes of a 19th-century vicar.
Emma	You're… you're Reverend Cameron. Caitlin?
	Emma begins to cry.
Danny	[*At the top of his voice*] Go away! Go away, I said.
	Danny swings again and misses again. Reverend Cameron undoes his neck tie, pulls his shirt away from his throat, tilts his head back and exposes his neck, which is a mass of red wheals and black and purple bruising.
Man/Rev. Cameron	Observe! What are these marks? They hanged me. They hanged me and I let them because I was protecting Eliza. And now you need protecting from her. She is coming for you. To her, you are one of the girls that caused all this. Make no mistake, she has lured you here. Come! You must come with me now!
Zack	Go away!
Emma	[*Clutching **Caitlin**'s arm*] What if it's all true? The dreams. They were about something in the house that wanted to kill me.
Caitlin	And he heard us talking about the dreams, and heard our names and knows the body snatcher story and has made up his own horror story to frighten us. We go back inside and wait to be found in the morning. [*Then, rounding on **Reverend Cameron***] Look what you've done to her, you sick man. You said you would leave if we asked you to. Now leave.
Man/Rev. Cameron	Very well. I have done all I can. But remember. Her power is greatest in the house, where her bones lie.
	Reverend Cameron turns and exits through the gate.

SCENE 2

Back in the vicarage. **Zack, Danny, Caitlin** *and* **Emma** *are sitting in a circle.* **Danny** *is still clutching the spade.*

Emma	I still think we should go.
Caitlin	We can't go. There's Zack's ankle, and the storm could start up again. And there's that horrible man.
Emma	But what if he wasn't making it up?
Zack	Look, Emma, I know it's been a really freaky night, but no one is coming to get you. Come on. Just try to remember what's real!
Emma	It's not you this ghost has sworn to kill!
Caitlin	But it's not real, Emma. You know ghosts aren't real.
Emma	How do I know? How do any of us know?
Danny	Oh, I've had enough of this.

Danny puts down the spade and walks over to the desk. He shoves it across the floor to the wall, and retrieves the spade.

Caitlin	What are you doing?
Danny	I'm going to prove to you that it was a story. If that man was telling the truth there will be a bag of money and a skeleton down there. *[Points to the floor]* Do any of you really think that's what I'll find if I pull up the floorboards?
Emma	No, Danny, don't!
Danny	It's the only way to prove it to you. Then you won't be so freaked out. Come on! We've got to know one way or the other.

Danny sticks the corner of the spade between two floorboards and a section of one of them pops out easily. He tries the boards on either side of the one that has come free, but neither will budge. He kneels down and reaches into the floor. He freezes.

Then, slowly, he pulls his hand back out of the floor. He is holding a human skull.

[Very shakily] I don't know... I don't know how this can be...

Emma	I knew it. Let's get out of here. Please!
Zack	Yeah, let's get out.

The knocking and scratching sounds start again. **Danny** *drops the skull.*

Emma It's happening. It's coming for us. Why did we stay here?

*They run—***Zack** *hobbles—to the window.* **Emma** *gets there first. She turns back to face the room, terrified.*

It's coming from out there! The noise is coming from outside as well!

Zack Quick, what should we do? Think! Think! Come on!

But before anyone voices a plan the knocking reaches a crescendo and with a loud splintering noise two more floorboards are thrown up in the air and **Eliza** *crawls out of the floor, her face completely white. She stands, shakes herself, looks slowly around the room, and seeing* **Zack, Danny, Caitlin** *and* **Emma** *by the window, she raises both arms in mock welcome.*

Eliza You came! How...wonderful!

Danny	We haven't done anything to hurt you. Let us go.
Eliza	*[Staring at **Emma**]* No. You have done nothing to hurt me. *[She bends down and picks up the skull]* Although who detached this from my spine?
Danny	*[Hoarsely]* Well…
Eliza	*[Still to **Emma**]* You separated my head from the rest of my body? But no, you have done nothing to hurt me. *[She drops the skull]* But Emma! You heard me calling and you came. How very sweet of you, my darling.
Caitlin	Leave her alone, please!
Eliza	Emma, my darling. Stay by the window, where you are now. I will clear some space.

*She beckons with a finger and **Zack**, **Caitlin** and **Danny** walk forwards to stand in front of **Eliza**.*

Danny	I'm not doing this. What's happening? I'm not walking.
Zack	She's doing it!

***Eliza** gives a flick with her hand and the three stumble backwards into three corners of the room, where they remain pressed up into the corners, twitching, unable to move forward.*

Emma	*[Trembling]* Oh God! Oh my God!

***Eliza** holds a finger to her lips. She walks slowly towards **Emma**, who is whimpering, and places a hand on each of her shoulders, staring into her eyes.*

Eliza	This could have ended happily, but because of the Barkers I was abandoned by the only people who loved me. And because of that, you must pay, darling. The same way my father paid. The same way Samuel paid. With… your… life!
Emma	*[Desperately]* But they… they didn't abandon you. Samuel loved you; he just didn't want to leave his family. Your father loved you so much he let them hang him because he thought you would go free.

Eliza	VERMIN! I swore I would not rest until I had my revenge. I did not lie.

Eliza puts her hands around Emma's throat and begins to squeeze. As she does so, the others find they can move. Everyone is screaming and shouting. Danny, Zack and Caitlin rush over to Emma but they cannot get Eliza off her.

Danny	The bones! The old man said she was powerful in the house because her bones are here. Zack, empty your bag. [*Zack hobbles over to his bag and empties it out on the floor*] Caitlin, get outside, get through the window. I'll pass the bones to you. You throw them as far away from the house as you can.

Caitlin does so and Danny and Zack frantically stuff bones from the hole in the floor into Zack's bag. All the while Eliza is continuing to choke Emma. Danny rushes to the window and passes the bag out.

Danny	Get rid of them!

Eliza lets out a huge sigh and slumps forward, rolling off Emma, who sits up spluttering and crying. Caitlin climbs back in. She and the boys haul Emma over to the other side of the room, opposite to where Eliza lies near the window. Slowly, Eliza gets to her feet. She looks at Emma for a few seconds.

Eliza	I will find you, Emma. I will not rest!

She climbs through the window, and is gone.

Act 4

• •

SCENE 1

A large, sunlit garden. Birdsong can be heard. There are two empty chairs facing each other in the middle of the garden. Dr Miller and Emma enter and walk towards the chairs. Dr Miller is wearing a white lab coat and is carrying a clipboard or notebook. In his pockets he has a pen, a mobile phone and business cards. Emma is wearing easily recognizable clothes and carrying a spade.

Dr Miller	Emma, good to talk to you again. Do have a seat.

Emma walks over and sits in one of the chairs, resting the spade against it, while Dr Miller sits opposite.

Dr Miller	Now, how have you been finding your time at the clinic?
Emma	It's OK, I guess, but I want to go home.
Dr Miller	And soon you will, Emma, I'm sure, but of course we need to be certain that you are quite well when you do go home, don't we?
Emma	I guess.
Dr Miller	Your parents have been in visiting every morning, haven't they?
Emma	Yes.
Dr Miller	Good. And what have you been doing today?
Emma	I've been helping here in the garden. Digging mostly. Why are we talking outside today?
Dr Miller	I just thought a change of scene might help. Now tell me, how have you been feeling?
Emma	[Shrugging] OK, I guess.
Dr Miller	Really?

Emma	Well, yeah. I'm still scared. But I'm OK.
Dr Miller	And what are you afraid of, Emma?
Emma	Well, that night in the house… You can't just forget about something like that.
Dr Miller	And just remind me, what happened that night? Where were you? Who were you with?
Emma	We've talked about this already, haven't we?
Dr Miller	Nonetheless. Just remind me.
Emma	Well, we were on a school trip up in the hills and a group of us got lost. Me, Danny, Zack and Caitlin. We got lost and it was getting dark and the weather was quite stormy. And I had this weird feeling, like I knew where to go even though I was lost.
Dr Miller	*[Leaning forward]* Tell me more about that weird feeling, Emma.
Emma	I…I don't know. I just sort of knew where to go. It was a bit like being in a dream where you can tell where you have to go. Even though you might not want to go there, you go there anyway.
Dr Miller	A bit like a dream?
Emma	Yeah, I guess.
Dr Miller	Go on.
Emma	Well, I was leading the way and we came to this house in the middle of nowhere. It had a graveyard next to it, and then I felt really weird because I'd seen the place in a dream before. Haven't we already talked about this?
Dr Miller	Maybe, but just tell me again anyway. What did you do when you got there?
Emma	We broke into the house to get out of the storm for the night. We spent the night there.
	She shivers.

Dr Miller	And what happened that night?
Emma	Do I have to? We've already talked about this. Why are we doing it all over again? Do I really have to?
Dr Miller	It would be best, yes.
Emma	Oh… *[Pause]* A man came to the house and told us a ghost story. All about how once there was a murder at the house, and a body snatcher. This girl, Eliza, wanted to run off with her boyfriend, so she was digging up the bodies and selling them. Then her boyfriend changed his mind, so she killed him. Her dad took the blame for it. But she got stuck hiding under the floorboards in the house, so they all died anyway.
Dr Miller	And this man… did he have a name?

Emma stands up and begins to pace up and down, facing away from Dr Miller.

| Emma | He said…this sounds so stupid. He said he was the ghost of Eliza's dad, Reverend Cameron. But it's not stupid. We told him to go away and he did, and then Eliza's ghost came out of the floor and tried to kill me. But the others threw her bones away and she disappeared. I've told you all this. I know it sounds crazy, but it's what happened. Why do we keep going over it? How am I ever going to get it out of my head if we keep talking about it all the time? |

Enter Caitlin, carrying a file and dressed as a nurse. She walks silently over to Dr Miller. Emma does not see her.

| Caitlin | *[Handing the file over]* That file for you, Dr Miller. |
| Dr Miller | Thank you, Caitlin. |

Emma starts at this, and looks round but by the time she does so Caitlin is walking away, her back to Emma the whole time.

	Right. Emma, I want you to talk to me a bit more about your dreams. Is that OK?
Emma	OK.
Dr Miller	Why don't you start with the recurring dream you had

	before that night – the one where you dreamed about the house before you'd ever been there?
Emma	*[Shivers]* OK. I am standing outside the house. Someone is watching me, but I can't see anyone. I feel sick. I want to run away, but I can't. I just have to stand where I am. This scratching sound starts, like something scratching wood. It keeps getting louder and louder and louder. Someone is trying to escape from something, and I know that whatever it is hates me. And then I see I'm in a graveyard, and I open my mouth to scream. That's when I wake up.
Dr Miller	Good, good.
Emma	Good? Not if you're me it isn't. And it gets worse.
Dr Miller	How do you mean worse?
Emma	After that night the dreams got worse.
Dr Miller	Go on.
Emma	I started dreaming that I am in the house, trying to escape. I am the one watching. I am the one who wants to kill someone. I never know who it is I want to kill. It's like I'm not me any more, like I've become someone else. It's me thinking. I'm there. But it's someone else's personality. It's the most horrible scary feeling. But anyway, you know all this. You asked me before.
Dr Miller	That's true.
Emma	So why are you asking me again?
Dr Miller	Emma, you can obviously remember that we spoke about the dreams before?
Emma	Yes.
Dr Miller	And do you remember how often?
Emma	Lots of times.
Dr Miller	Yes, and do you remember what I say to you after each time we have this discussion?

Emma	What do you mean?
Dr Miller	*[Sighs and rubs his eyes]* I can see we are going to have to start again. Listen carefully. There was no school trip, Emma. You were there by yourself. Nobody knows how you got there. You were found the next morning by a passing rambler, Mr Howard. Something happened that night that terrified you, and since then you have become confused about what is real and what is not. You did go to the house. There was a storm. You did break in and spend the night there. But you were alone.

Emma stares at Dr Miller and begins to fidget in a very agitated way.

Emma, I know this is very difficult for you to understand, but you need to break this cycle. Your dreams are very vivid, I understand that. But they are dreams.

Emma	This is stupid. I shouldn't have told you anything. Whenever I talk about this to anyone they think I'm crazy, but I'm not. THIS STUFF HAPPENED!
Dr Miller	Emma, who were the friends who were with you that night?
Emma	*[Defensively]* Zack, Danny and Caitlin.
Dr Miller	Emma, turn around and look back at the main building for me, would you?

She turns and looks offstage.

You see those two boys by the doors? One with a bandaged leg. They look like they're arguing about something. Look closely. Do you recognize either of them?

Emma	That's... that's impossible.
Dr Miller	No, it's real. What are their names, Emma?
Emma	*[Shocked]* Zack and Danny.

Dr Miller leads Emma back to the chair and they sit down again.

Dr Miller	That's right. They were here at the clinic that night when you were in the house. You had never met them until after you were rescued. Now look at me, Emma. What is my name?
Emma	You're Dr… *[She falters]* I don't remember your name.
	He leans forward and hands her a business card.
Dr Miller	Look. Please read out what you see written on the card.
Emma	Dr Samuel Miller.
	She drops the card and holds her hands over her mouth.
Dr Miller	Emma, can you see what has happened? You have made a story up. It's not your fault; you are not doing it deliberately. It is a story you believe in totally. Perhaps you dreamed it. Perhaps your subconscious has created it to rationalize the experience of that night in the house. I can't say for sure. Your mind has taken some of the influences in your life here and spun them into the story. Samuel Miller, Zack and Danny, Caitlin too, the one who looked after you. She's a nurse here. And the gravedigging, the spade. What were you doing in the garden today, and indeed on many other occasions before today? Digging, Emma. Digging with a spade.
Emma	But…but what about Eliza? What about Reverend Cameron?
Dr Miller	I don't know, Emma. You have told me so many details that I looked some of them up. There was once a Reverend Cameron at Caldmere, and he did have a daughter named Eliza. There was a murder story. Maybe you heard about these somewhere. Maybe you found something in the house that gave you the basics of the story. I don't know, and you can't remember.
Emma	*[Starting to panic]* I… I don't know… I don't know what to do. What should I do?
Dr Miller	You just need to try and focus on what I have told you. Try and hold on to the thought that the story was just that – a

ACT 4   SCENE 1

story, a work of fiction. However real it still seems, it will start to fade the longer you can hold on to the idea that it is pure fiction. Will you try and do that for me?

She nods her head quickly without speaking.

Good. Now I need…

*A mobile phone rings. **Dr Miller** excuses himself, answers the phone, stands and turns away from **Emma**.*

Dr Miller speaking.

***Emma** stares around at her surroundings and puts a hand over her mouth.*

I'm with someone at the moment, is this absolutely urgent?

*Suddenly **Emma** throws herself back in her chair wide-eyed, clutching her throat with both hands, throttling herself. Her whole body shakes as if she is having some kind of fit, then goes limp. Her hands fall away from her throat. Slowly, looking blank, she sits up very straight in the chair.*

Emma	*[In a hoarse whisper]* I will not rest.
Dr Miller	Yes, yes, just calm down. I'll be there as soon as I can.
Emma	*[Still hoarse]* This could have ended happily.

***Dr Miller** hangs up and turns back to face **Emma**.*

Dr Miller	Right, now where were we?
Emma	*[Clears her throat and speaks loudly]* You were telling me what to believe, Dr Miller.
Dr Miller	*[Taken aback by her change in tone]* Yes. Yes, I was. Listen, Emma, we'll talk again tomorrow, OK? For now just try to remember what I told you. However real it might seem, none of the things you are afraid of are real. OK? I think we're making progress, you know. You seem quite different now compared to how you have been at the end of our other sessions.
Emma	Is this really the end, Dr Miller?

Dr Miller	Well, yes, for now. I really think we've known each other long enough that you could refer to me... Oh, never mind. Yes, for now this is the end. Next time we meet we will pick up where we left off.

Silently, **Emma** *stands up and exits stiffly, taking the spade with her.* **Dr Miller** *looks after her for a moment and shakes his head. He looks down and starts writing in the file.*

Still delusional... Still believes in the haunting... Some interesting reactions today... On the subject of her dreams, interesting point about feeling like she was someone else... Could be something in that... Look back at similar cases... Must probe further in future sessions...

There is a scraping sound for a few seconds. Then **Eliza** *appears, dragging the spade across the floor, her face completely white as before. She is wearing Emma's clothes. She advances slowly across the stage towards* **Dr Miller** *until she is standing directly behind him.*

Dr Miller	*[Still writing]* ...Seemed unusually strong at the end of the session, stronger than ever...

Eliza *raises the spade aloft, throws back her head and screams the words...*

Eliza	I WILL NOT REST!

Blackout

'THE BODY SNATCHER' BY ROBERT LOUIS STEVENSON

Introduction

Robert Louis Stevenson was born in Edinburgh in 1850 and died in Samoa in 1894, aged 44. During Stevenson's short life, he travelled the world and pursued his passion for writing. His much-loved first novel, *Treasure Island*, was published in 1883 and has since never been out of print. Stevenson finally achieved worldwide success with his chilling tale, *The Strange Case of Dr Jekyll and Mr Hyde* (1886).

When Stevenson first wrote 'The Body Snatcher' it was deemed too terrifying to publish, even for adult readers! A few years later, a London magazine decided to publish the story and it was devoured by fans who were delighted by its dark and haunting tones – as we have been ever since. In fact, I was so delighted that I wanted to replicate some of the feel of this story when I wrote *Flesh and Blood*.

You may notice that the play 'borrows' certain things from the story: Fettes and Macfarlane are the young body snatchers in the story; there is a murder; there is a ghost; there is an ethical debate about body-snatching – ghoulish horror on one hand, medical necessity on the other. Best of all, there is a brilliantly set up and truly horrifying twist at the end.

To Stevenson, the appeal of horror lay in the impact that the horrifying event had on human character. 'The Body Snatcher' is a wonderful example of a story that includes a hint of the supernatural but conveys all the horror through the reactions of the characters. Real people, driven to the edge of insanity by fear. Now that's horror.

Benjamin Hulme-Cross

'The Body Snatcher' by Robert Louis Stevenson

Every night in the year, four of us sat in the small parlour of the George at Debenham — the undertaker, and the landlord, and Fettes, and myself. Sometimes there would be more; but blow high, blow low, come rain or snow or frost, we four would be each planted in his own particular armchair. Fettes was an old drunken Scotsman, a man of education obviously, and a man of some property, since he lived in idleness. He had come to Debenham years ago, while still young, and by a mere continuance of living had grown to be an adopted townsman. His blue camlet cloak was a local antiquity, like the church spire. His place in the parlour at the George, his absence from church, his old, **crapulous**[1], disreputable vices, were all things of course in Debenham. He had some vague Radical opinions and some fleeting **infidelities**[2], which he would now and again set forth and emphasise with tottering slaps upon the table. He drank rum — five glasses regularly every evening; and for the greater portion of his nightly visit to the George sat, with his glass in his right hand, in a state of melancholy alcoholic saturation. We called him the Doctor, for he was supposed to have some special knowledge of medicine, and had been known, upon a pinch, to set a fracture or reduce a dislocation; but, beyond these slight particulars, we had no knowledge of his character and **antecedents**[3].

One dark winter night — it had struck nine some time before the landlord joined us — there was a sick man in the George, a great neighbouring proprietor suddenly struck down with **apoplexy**[4] on his way to Parliament; and the great man's still greater London doctor had been telegraphed to his bedside. It was the first time that such a thing had happened in Debenham, for the railway was but newly open, and we were all proportionately moved by the occurrence.

---

1. **crapulous** – drunken
2. **infidelities** – belief that God does not exist
3. **antecedents** – family history
4. **apoplexy** – a stroke

'He's come,' said the landlord, after he had filled and lighted his pipe.

'He?' said I. 'Who? — not the doctor?'

'Himself,' replied our host.

'What is his name?'

'Dr Macfarlane,' said the landlord.

Fettes was far through his third tumbler, stupidly fuddled, now nodding over, now staring mazily around him; but at the last word he seemed to awaken, and repeated the name 'Macfarlane' twice, quietly enough the first time, but with sudden emotion at the second.

'Yes,' said the landlord, 'that's his name, Dr Wolfe Macfarlane.'

Fettes became instantly sober; his eyes awoke, his voice became clear, loud, and steady, his language forcible and earnest. We were all startled by the transformation, as if a man had risen from the dead.

'I beg your pardon,' he said; 'I am afraid I have not been paying much attention to your talk. Who is this Wolfe Macfarlane?' And then, when he had heard the landlord out, 'It cannot be, it cannot be,' he added; 'and yet I would like well to see him face to face.'

'Do you know him, Doctor?' asked the undertaker, with a gasp.

'God forbid!' was the reply. 'And yet the name is a strange one; it were too much to fancy two. Tell me, landlord, is he old?'

'Well,' said the host, 'he's not a young man, to be sure, and his hair is white; but he looks younger than you.'

'He is older, though; years older. But,' with a slap upon the table, 'it's the rum you see in my face — rum and sin. This man, perhaps, may have an easy conscience and a good digestion. Conscience! Hear me speak. You would think I was some good, old, decent Christian, would you not? But no, not I; I never **canted**[5]. Voltaire might have canted if he'd stood in my shoes; but the brains' — with a rattling fillip on his bald

---

5. canted – talked hypocritically or self-righteously

head — 'the brains were clear and active, and I saw and made no deductions.'

'If you know this doctor,' I ventured to remark, after a somewhat awful pause, 'I should gather that you do not share the landlord's good opinion.'

Fettes paid no regard to me.

'Yes,' he said, with sudden decision, 'I must see him face to face.'

There was another pause, and then a door was closed rather sharply on the first floor, and a step was heard upon the stair.

'That's the doctor,' cried the landlord. 'Look sharp, and you can catch him.'

It was but two steps from the small parlour to the door of the old George Inn; the wide oak staircase landed almost in the street; there was room for a Turkey rug and nothing more between the threshold and the last round of the descent; but this little space was every evening brilliantly lit up, not only by the light upon the stair and the great signal-lamp below the sign, but by the warm radiance of the bar-room window. The George thus brightly advertised itself to passers-by in the cold street. Fettes walked steadily to the spot, and we, who were hanging behind, beheld the two men meet, as one of them had phrased it, face to face. Dr Macfarlane was alert and vigorous. His white hair set off his pale and placid, although energetic, countenance. He was richly dressed in the finest of broadcloth and the whitest of linen, with a great gold watch-chain, and studs and spectacles of the same precious material. He wore a broad-folded tie, white and speckled with lilac, and he carried on his arm a comfortable driving-coat of fur. There was no doubt but he became his years, breathing, as he did, of wealth and consideration; and it was a surprising contrast to see our parlour sot — bald, dirty, pimpled, and robed in his old camlet cloak — confront him at the bottom of the stairs.

'Macfarlane!' he said somewhat loudly, more like a **herald**[6] than a friend.

---

6. **herald** – an official

The great doctor pulled up short on the fourth step, as though the familiarity of the address surprised and somewhat shocked his dignity.

'Toddy Macfarlane!' repeated Fettes.

The London man almost staggered. He stared for the swiftest of seconds at the man before him, glanced behind him with a sort of scare, and then in a startled whisper, 'Fettes!' he said, 'you!'

'Ay,' said the other, 'me! Did you think I was dead, too? We are not so easy shut of our acquaintance.'

'Hush, hush!' exclaimed the doctor. 'Hush, hush! this meeting is so unexpected — I can see you are unmanned. I hardly knew you, I confess, at first; but I am overjoyed — overjoyed to have this opportunity. For the present it must be how-d'ye-do and goodbye in one, for my fly is waiting, and I must not fail the train; but you shall — let me see — yes — you shall give me your address, and you can count on early news of me. We must do something for you, Fettes. I fear you are out at elbows; but we must see to that for auld lang syne, as once we sang at suppers.'

'Money!' cried Fettes; 'money from you! The money that I had from you is lying where I cast it in the rain.'

Dr Macfarlane had talked himself into some measure of superiority and confidence, but the uncommon energy of this refusal cast him back into his first confusion.

A horrible, ugly look came and went across his almost venerable countenance. 'My dear fellow,' he said, 'be it as you please; my last thought is to offend you. I would intrude on none. I will leave you my address, however —'

'I do not wish it — I do not wish to know the roof that shelters you,' interrupted the other. 'I heard your name; I feared it might be you; I wished to know if, after all, there were a God; I know now that there is none. Begone!'

He still stood in the middle of the rug, between the stair and doorway; and the great London physician, in order to escape, would be forced to step to one side. It was plain that he hesitated before the thought of this humiliation. White as he was, there was a dangerous glitter in his spectacles; but, while he still paused uncertain, he became aware that the driver of his fly was peering in from the street at this unusual scene, and caught a glimpse at the same time of our little body from the parlour, huddled by the corner of the bar. The presence of so many witnesses decided him at once to flee. He crouched together, brushing on the **wainscot**[7], and made a dart like a serpent, striking for the door. But his **tribulation**[8] was not yet entirely at an end, for even as he was passing Fettes clutched him by the arm and these words came in a whisper, and yet painfully distinct, 'Have you seen it again?'

The great rich London doctor cried out aloud with a sharp, throttling cry; he dashed his questioner across the open space, and, with his hands over his head, fled out of the door like a detected thief. Before it had occurred to one of us to make a movement the fly was already rattling toward the station. The scene was over like a dream, but the dream had left proofs and traces of its passage. Next day the servant found the fine gold spectacles broken on the threshold, and that very night we were all standing breathless by the barroom window, and Fettes at our side, sober, pale, and resolute in look.

'God protect us, Mr Fettes!' said the landlord, coming first into possession of his customary senses. 'What in the universe is all this? These are strange things you have been saying.'

Fettes turned toward us; he looked us each in succession in the face. 'See if you can hold your tongues,' said he. 'That man Macfarlane is not safe to cross; those that have done so already have repented it too late.'

And then, without so much as finishing his third glass, far less waiting for the other two, he bade us goodbye and went forth, under the lamp of the hotel, into the black night.

We three turned to our places in the parlour, with the big red fire and four clear candles; and, as we **recapitulated**[9] what had passed, the first chill of our surprise soon changed into

---

7. **wainscot** – wooden panelling on the bottom half of a wall
8. **tribulation** – trouble or suffering
9. **recapitulated** – repeated and summarized

a glow of curiosity. We sat late; it was the latest session I have known in the old George. Each man, before we parted, had his theory that he was bound to prove; and none of us had any nearer business in this world than to track out the past of our condemned companion, and surprise the secret that he shared with the great London doctor. It is no great boast, but I believe I was a better hand at worming out a story than either of my fellows at the George; and perhaps there is now no other man alive who could narrate to you the following foul and unnatural events.

In his young days Fettes studied medicine in the schools of Edinburgh. He had talent of a kind, the talent that picks up swiftly what it hears and readily **retails**[10] it for its own. He worked little at home; but he was civil, attentive, and intelligent in the presence of his masters. They soon picked him out as a lad who listened closely and remembered well; nay, strange as it seemed to me when I first heard it, he was in those days well favoured, and pleased by his exterior. There was, at that period, a certain **extramural**[11] teacher of **anatomy**[12], whom I shall here designate by the letter K. His name was subsequently too well known. The man who bore it skulked through the streets of Edinburgh in disguise, while the mob that applauded at the execution of Burke called loudly for the blood of his employer. But Mr K—— was then at the top of his **vogue**[13]; he enjoyed a popularity due partly to his own talent and address, partly to the incapacity of his rival, the university professor. The students, at least, swore by his name, and Fettes believed himself, and was believed by others, to have laid the foundations of success when he had acquired the favour of this meteorically famous man. Mr K—— was a ***bon vivant***[14] as well as an accomplished teacher; he liked a sly

---

10. **retails** – passes it on
11. **extramural** – not attached to the university in a full-time or core capacity
12. **anatomy** – the scientific study of the structure of the bodies of humans and animals, usually through dissection
13. **vogue** – popularity or fashionableness
14. **bon vivant** – someone who enjoys the high life

illusion no less than a careful preparation. In both capacities Fettes enjoyed and deserved his notice, and by the second year of his attendance he held the half-regular position of second demonstrator or sub-assistant in his class.

In this capacity the charge of the theatre and lecture-room **devolved**[15] in particular upon his shoulders. He had to answer for the cleanliness of the premises and the conduct of the other students, and it was a part of his duty to supply, receive, and divide the various subjects. It was with a view to this last — at that time very delicate — affair that he was lodged by Mr K—— in the same **wynd**[16], and at last in the same building, with the dissecting-rooms. Here, after a night of turbulent pleasures, his hand still tottering, his sight still misty and confused, he would be called out of bed in the black hours before the winter dawn by the unclean and desperate **interlopers**[17] who supplied the table. He would open the door to these men, since infamous throughout the land. He would help them with their tragic burden, pay them their sordid price, and remain alone, when they were gone, with the unfriendly relics of humanity. From such a scene he would return to snatch another hour or two of slumber, to repair the abuses of the night, and refresh himself for the labours of the day.

Few lads could have been more insensible to the impressions of a life thus passed among the **ensigns**[18] of mortality. His mind was closed against all general considerations. He was incapable of interest in the fate and fortunes of another, the slave of his own desires and low ambitions. Cold, light, and selfish in the last resort, he had that modicum of prudence, miscalled morality which keeps a man from inconvenient drunkenness or punishable theft. He coveted, besides, a measure of consideration from his masters and his fellow-pupils, and he had no desire to fail conspicuously in the

---

15. **devolved upon his shoulders** – was handed over to him
16. **wynd** – a narrow street or alley
17. **interlopers** – accomplices who do not seem to belong or are out of place
18. **ensigns** – symbols

external parts of life. Thus he made it his pleasure to gain some distinction in his studies, and day after day rendered **unimpeachable**[19] eye-service to his employer, Mr K——. For his day of work he **indemnified**[20] himself by nights of roaring, blackguardly enjoyment; and when that balance had been struck, the organ that he called his conscience declared itself content.

The supply of subjects was a continual trouble to him as well as to his master. In that large and busy class, the raw material of the anatomists kept perpetually running out; and the business thus rendered necessary was not only unpleasant in itself, but threatened dangerous consequences to all who were concerned. It was the policy of Mr K—— to ask no questions in his dealings with the trade. 'They bring the body, and we pay the price,' he used to say, dwelling on the alliteration — '*quid pro quo*'[21]. And, again, and somewhat **profanely**[22], 'Ask no questions,' he would tell his assistants, 'for conscience' sake.' There was no understanding that the subjects were provided by the crime of murder. Had that idea been broached to him in words, he would have recoiled in horror; but the lightness of his speech upon so grave a matter was, in itself, an offence against good manners, and a temptation to the men with whom he dealt. Fettes, for instance, had often remarked to himself upon the singular freshness of the bodies. He had been struck again and again by the hang-dog, abominable looks of the ruffians who came to him before the dawn; and, putting things together clearly in his private thoughts, he perhaps attributed a meaning too immoral and too categorical to the unguarded **counsels**[23] of his master. He understood his duty, in short, to have three branches: to take what was brought, to pay the price, and to avert the eye from any evidence of crime.

---

19. unimpeachable – not to be doubted, completely trustworthy
20. indemnified – compensated, made up for
21. 'quid pro quo' – a favour given in return for something; the Latin translation is 'something for something'
22. profanely – disrespectfully, flippantly
23. counsels – advice

One November morning this policy of silence was put sharply to the test. He had been awake all night with a racking toothache — pacing his room like a caged beast or throwing himself in fury on his bed — and had fallen at last into that profound, uneasy slumber that so often follows on a night of pain, when he was awakened by the third or fourth angry repetition of the concerted signal. There was a thin, bright moonshine; it was bitter cold, windy, and frosty; the town had not yet awakened, but an indefinable stir already **preluded**[24] the noise and business of the day. The ghouls had come later than usual, and they seemed more than usually eager to be gone. Fettes, sick with sleep, lighted them upstairs. He heard their grumbling Irish voices through a dream; and as they stripped the sack from their sad merchandise he leaned dozing, with his shoulder propped against the wall; he had to shake himself to find the men their money. As he did so his eyes lighted on the dead face. He started; he took two steps nearer, with the candle raised.

'God Almighty!' he cried. 'That is Jane Galbraith!'

The men answered nothing, but they shuffled nearer the door.

'I know her, I tell you,' he continued. 'She was alive and hearty yesterday. It's impossible she can be dead; it's impossible you should have got this body fairly.'

'Sure, sir, you're mistaken entirely,' said one of the men.

But the other looked Fettes darkly in the eyes, and demanded the money on the spot.

It was impossible to misconceive the threat or to exaggerate the danger. The lad's heart failed him. He stammered some excuses, counted out the sum, and saw his hateful visitors depart. No sooner were they gone than he hastened to confirm his doubts. By a dozen unquestionable marks he identified the girl he had jested with the day before. He saw, with horror, marks upon her body that might well betoken violence. A panic seized him, and he took refuge in his room. There he reflected

24. **preluded** – introduced, gave a taste of

at length over the discovery that he had made; considered soberly the bearing of Mr K——'s instructions and the danger to himself of interference in so serious a business, and at last, in sore **perplexity**[25], determined to wait for the advice of his immediate superior, the class assistant.

This was a young doctor, Wolfe Macfarlane, a high favourite among all the reckless students, clever, **dissipated**[26], and **unscrupulous**[27] to the last degree. He had travelled and studied abroad. His manners were agreeable and a little forward. He was an authority on the stage, skilful on the ice or the links with skate or golf-club; he dressed with nice **audacity**[28], and, to put the finishing touch upon his glory, he kept a **gig**[29] and a strong trotting-horse. With Fettes he was on terms of intimacy; indeed, their relative positions called for some community of life; and when subjects were scarce the pair would drive far into the country in Macfarlane's gig, visit and **desecrate**[30] some lonely graveyard, and return before dawn with their booty to the door of the dissecting-room.

On that particular morning Macfarlane arrived somewhat earlier than his **wont**[31]. Fettes heard him, and met him on the stairs, told him his story, and showed him the cause of his alarm. Macfarlane examined the marks on her body.

'Yes,' he said with a nod, 'it looks fishy.'

'Well, what should I do?' asked Fettes.

'Do?' repeated the other. 'Do you want to do anything? Least said soonest mended, I should say.'

'Someone else might recognise her,' objected Fettes. 'She was as well known as the Castle Rock.'

'We'll hope not,' said Macfarlane, 'and if anybody does — well, you didn't, don't you see, and there's an end. The fact is,

---

25. perplexity – confusion
26. dissipated – overindulging in the high life
27. unscrupulous – dishonest, immoral
28. audacity – boldness, with a devil-may-care attitude
29. gig – a light carriage with two wheels and pulled by one horse
30. desecrate – dishonour, damage (a sacred thing or place)
31. wont – habit, usual behaviour

this has been going on too long. Stir up the mud, and you'll get K—— into the most unholy trouble; you'll be in a shocking box yourself. So will I, if you come to that. I should like to know how any one of us would look, or what the devil we should have to say for ourselves, in any Christian witness-box. For me, you know, there's one thing certain — that, practically speaking, all our subjects have been murdered.'

'Macfarlane!' cried Fettes.

'Come now!' sneered the other. 'As if you hadn't suspected it yourself!'

'Suspecting is one thing —'

'And proof another. Yes, I know; and I'm as sorry as you are this should have come here,' tapping the body with his cane. 'The next best thing for me is not to recognise it; and,' he added coolly, 'I don't. You may, if you please. I don't dictate, but I think a man of the world would do as I do; and, I may add, I fancy that is what K—— would look for at our hands. The question is, Why did he choose us two for his assistants? And I answer, Because he didn't want old wives.'

This was the tone of all others to affect the mind of a lad like Fettes. He agreed to imitate Macfarlane. The body of the unfortunate girl was duly dissected, and no one remarked or appeared to recognise her.

One afternoon, when his day's work was over, Fettes dropped into a popular tavern and found Macfarlane sitting with a stranger. This was a small man, very pale and dark, with coal-black eyes. The cut of his features gave a promise of intellect and refinement which was but feebly realised in his manners, for he proved, upon a nearer acquaintance, coarse, vulgar, and stupid. He exercised, however, a very remarkable control over Macfarlane; issued orders like the Great Bashaw; became inflamed at the least discussion or delay, and commented rudely on the servility with which he was obeyed. This most offensive person took a fancy to Fettes on the spot, plied him with drinks, and honoured him with unusual confidences on his past career. If a tenth part of what he confessed were true, he was a very loathsome rogue; and the lad's vanity was tickled by the attention of so experienced a man.

'I'm a pretty bad fellow myself,' the stranger remarked, 'but Macfarlane is the boy — Toddy Macfarlane I call him. Toddy, order your friend another glass.' Or it might be, 'Toddy, you jump up and shut the door.' 'Toddy hates me,' he said again. 'Oh, yes, Toddy, you do!'

'Don't you call me that confounded name,' growled Macfarlane.

'Hear him! Did you ever see the lads play knife? He would like to do that all over my body,' remarked the stranger.

'We medicals have a better way than that,' said Fettes. 'When we dislike a dead friend of ours, we dissect him.'

Macfarlane looked up sharply, as though this jest were scarcely to his mind.

The afternoon passed. Gray, for that was the stranger's name, invited Fettes to join them at dinner, ordered a feast so sumptuous that the tavern was thrown into commotion, and when all was done commanded Macfarlane to settle the bill. It was late before they separated; the man Gray was incapably drunk. Macfarlane, sobered by his fury, **chewed the cud**[32] of the money he had been forced to squander and the slights he had been obliged to swallow. Fettes, with various liquors singing in his head, returned home with devious footsteps and a mind entirely **in abeyance**[33]. Next day Macfarlane was absent from the class, and Fettes smiled to himself as he imagined him still **squiring**[34] the intolerable Gray from tavern to tavern. As soon as the hour of liberty had struck, he posted from place to place in quest of his last night's companions. He could find them, however, nowhere; so returned early to his rooms, went early to bed, and slept the sleep of the just.

At four in the morning he was awakened by the well-known signal. Descending to the door, he was filled with astonishment to find Macfarlane with his gig, and in the gig one of those long and ghastly packages with which he was so well acquainted.

---

32. **chewed the cud** – thought deeply
33. **in abeyance** – suspended, not being used at that moment
34. **squiring** – accompanying

'What?' he cried. 'Have you been out alone? How did you manage?'

But Macfarlane silenced him roughly, bidding him turn to business. When they had got the body upstairs and laid it on the table, Macfarlane made at first as if he were going away. Then he paused and seemed to hesitate; and then, 'You had better look at the face,' said he, in tones of some constraint. 'You had better,' he repeated, as Fettes only stared at him in wonder.

'But where, and how, and when did you come by it?' cried the other.

'Look at the face,' was the only answer.

Fettes was staggered; strange doubts **assailed**[35] him. He looked from the young doctor to the body, and then back again. At last, with a start, he did as he was bidden. He had almost expected the sight that met his eyes, and yet the shock was cruel. To see, fixed in the rigidity of death and naked on that coarse layer of sackcloth, the man whom he had left well clad and full of meat and sin upon the threshold of a tavern, awoke, even in the thoughtless Fettes, some of the terrors of the conscience. It was a *cras tibi*[36] which re-echoed in his soul, that two whom he had known should have come to lie upon these icy tables. Yet these were only secondary thoughts. His first concern regarded Wolfe. Unprepared for a challenge so momentous, he knew not how to look his comrade in the face. He **durst**[37] not meet his eye, and he had neither words nor voice at his command.

It was Macfarlane himself who made the first advance. He came up quietly behind and laid his hand gently but firmly on the other's shoulder.

'Richardson,' said he, 'may have the head.'

Now, Richardson was a student who had long been anxious for that portion of the human subject to dissect. There was no

---

35. assailed – overwhelmed, usually by something unpleasant
36. cras tibi – a warning to the living from the dead that they will be next: 'tomorrow it will be you'
37. durst – dared

answer, and the murderer resumed: 'Talking of business, you must pay me; your accounts, you see, must tally.'

Fettes found a voice, the ghost of his own: 'Pay you!' he cried. 'Pay you for that?'

'Why, yes, of course you must. By all means and on every possible account, you must,' returned the other. 'I dare not give it for nothing, you dare not take it for nothing; it would compromise us both. This is another case like Jane Galbraith's. The more things are wrong, the more we must act as if all were right. Where does old K—— keep his money?'

'There,' answered Fettes hoarsely, pointing to a cupboard in the corner.

'Give me the key, then,' said the other calmly, holding out his hand.

There was an instant's hesitation, and the die was cast. Macfarlane could not suppress a nervous twitch, the **infinitesimal**[38] mark of an immense relief, as he felt the key between his fingers. He opened the cupboard, brought out pen and ink and a paper-book that stood in one compartment, and separated from the funds in a drawer a sum suitable to the occasion.

'Now, look here,' he said, 'there is the payment made — first proof of your good faith: first step to your security. You have now to clinch it by a second. Enter the payment in your book, and then you for your part may defy the devil.'

The next few seconds were for Fettes an agony of thought; but in balancing his terrors it was the most immediate that triumphed. Any future difficulty seemed almost welcome if he could avoid a present quarrel with Macfarlane. He set down the candle which he had been carrying all this time, and with a steady hand entered the date, the nature, and the amount of the transaction.

'And now,' said Macfarlane, 'it's only fair that you should pocket the **lucre**[39]. I've had my share already. By-the-by, when

---

38. infinitesimal – very small
39. lucre – money, although usually ill-gotten

a man of the world falls into a bit of luck, has a few shillings extra in his pocket — I'm ashamed to speak of it, but there's a rule of conduct in the case. No treating, no purchase of expensive class-books, no squaring of old debts; borrow, don't lend.'

'Macfarlane,' began Fettes, still somewhat hoarsely, 'I have put my neck in a halter to oblige you.'

'To oblige me?' cried Wolfe. 'Oh, come! You did, as near as I can see the matter, what you downright had to do in self-defence. Suppose I got into trouble, where would you be? This second little matter flows clearly from the first. Mr Gray is the continuation of Miss Galbraith. You can't begin and then stop. If you begin, you must keep on beginning; that's the truth. No rest for the wicked.'

A horrible sense of blackness and the treachery of fate seized hold upon the soul of the unhappy student.

'My God!' he cried, 'but what have I done? and when did I begin? To be made a class assistant — in the name of reason, where's the harm in that? Service wanted the position; Service might have got it. Would *he* have been where *I* am now?'

'My dear fellow,' said Macfarlane, 'what a boy you are! What harm *has* come to you? What harm *can* come to you if you hold your tongue? Why, man, do you know what this life is? There are two squads of us — the lions and the lambs. If you're a lamb, you'll come to lie upon these tables like Gray or Jane Galbraith; if you're a lion, you'll live and drive a horse like me, like K——, like all the world with any wit or courage. You're staggered at the first. But look at K——! My dear fellow, you're clever, you have pluck. I like you, and K—— likes you. You were born to lead the hunt; and I tell you, on my honour and my experience of life, three days from now you'll laugh at all these scarecrows like a High School boy at a farce.'

And with that Macfarlane took his departure and drove off up the wynd in his gig to get under cover before daylight. Fettes was thus left alone with his regrets. He saw the miserable peril in which he stood involved. He saw, with inexpressible dismay, that there was no limit to his weakness, and that, from concession[40] to concession, he had fallen from the **arbiter**[41] of Macfarlane's destiny to his paid and helpless accomplice. He would have given the world to have been a little braver at the time, but it did not occur to him that he might still be brave. The secret of Jane Galbraith and the cursed entry in the day-book closed his mouth.

Hours passed; the class began to arrive; the members of the unhappy Gray were dealt out to one and to another, and received without remark. Richardson was made happy with the head; and, before the hour of freedom rang, Fettes trembled with **exultation**[42] to perceive how far they had already gone toward safety.

For two days he continued to watch, with an increasing joy, the dreadful process of disguise.

On the third day Macfarlane made his appearance. He had been ill, he said; but he made up for lost time by the energy with which he directed the students. To Richardson in particular he extended the most valuable assistance and advice, and that student, encouraged by the praise of the demonstrator, burned high with ambitious hopes, and saw the medal already in his grasp.

Before the week was out Macfarlane's prophecy had been fulfilled. Fettes had outlived his terrors and had forgotten his baseness. He began to **plume**[43] himself upon his courage, and had so arranged the story in his mind that he could look back on these events with an unhealthy pride. Of his accomplice he saw but little. They met, of course, in the business of the class; they received their orders together from Mr K——. At times they had a word or two in private, and Macfarlane was from first to last particularly kind and jovial. But it was plain that he avoided any reference to their common secret; and even when Fettes whispered to him that he had cast in his lot with the lions

---

40. concession – the acceptance of something
41. arbiter – someone with influence and control
42. exultation – triumphant happiness
43. plume – feel a sense of self-satisfaction

and forsworn the lambs, he only signed to him smilingly to hold his peace.

At length an occasion arose which threw the pair once more into a closer union. Mr K—— was again short of subjects; pupils were eager, and it was a part of this teacher's **pretensions**[44] to be always well supplied. At the same time there came the news of a burial in the rustic graveyard of Glencorse. Time has little changed the place in question. It stood then, as now, upon a cross-road, out of call of human habitations, and buried fathoms deep in the foliage of six cedar-trees. The cries of the sheep upon the neighbouring hills, the streamlets upon either hand, one loudly singing among pebbles, the other dripping **furtively**[45] from pond to pond, the stir of the wind in mountainous old flowering chestnuts, and once in seven days the voice of the bell and the old tunes of the **precentor**[46], were the only sounds that disturbed the silence around the rural church. The Resurrection Man — to use a by-name of the period — was not to be **deterred**[47] by any of the **sanctities**[48] of customary **piety**[49]. It was part of his trade to despise and desecrate the scrolls and trumpets of old tombs, the paths worn by the feet of worshippers and mourners, and the offerings and the inscriptions of bereaved affection. To rustic neighbourhoods where love is more than commonly **tenacious**[50], and where some bonds of blood or fellowship unite the entire society of a parish, the body snatcher, far from being repelled by natural respect, was attracted by the ease and safety of the task. To bodies that had been laid in earth, in joyful expectation of a far different awakening, there came that hasty, lamp-lit, terror-haunted resurrection of the spade and

---

44. pretensions – claims to a – usually unjustified – reputation
45. furtively – secretively, guiltily avoiding notice
46. precentor – the person who leads the congregation's singing
47. deterred – put off
48. sanctities – things which are believed to be holy or sacred
49. piety – religiousness
50. tenacious – strong and unshakeable

mattock. The coffin was forced, the **cerements**[51] torn, and the melancholy relics, clad in sackcloth, after being rattled for hours on moonless by-ways, were at length exposed to uttermost indignities before a class of gaping boys.

Somewhat as two vultures may swoop upon a dying lamb, Fettes and Macfarlane were to be let loose upon a grave in that green and quiet resting-place. The wife of a farmer, a woman who had lived for sixty years, and been known for nothing but good butter and a godly conversation, was to be rooted from her grave at midnight and carried, dead and naked, to that far-away city that she had always honoured with her Sunday's best; the place beside her family was to be empty till the crack of doom; her innocent and almost venerable members to be exposed to that last curiosity of the anatomist.

Late one afternoon the pair set forth, well wrapped in cloaks and furnished with a formidable bottle. It rained without **remission**[52] — a cold, dense, lashing rain. Now and again there blew a puff of wind, but these sheets of falling water kept it down. Bottle and all, it was a sad and silent drive as far as Penicuik, where they were to spend the evening. They stopped once, to hide their implements in a thick bush not far from the churchyard, and once again at the Fisher's Tryst, to have a toast before the kitchen fire and vary their nips of whisky with a glass of ale. When they reached their journey's end the gig was housed, the horse was fed and comforted, and the two young doctors in a private room sat down to the best dinner and the best wine the house afforded. The lights, the fire, the beating rain upon the window, the cold, **incongruous**[53] work that lay before them, added zest to their enjoyment of the meal. With every glass their **cordiality**[54] increased. Soon Macfarlane handed a little pile of gold to his companion.

---

51. **cerements** – cloth used for wrapping a corpse in
52. **remission** – a pause or break
53. **incongruous** – out of keeping, contradictory
54. **cordiality** – friendliness

'A compliment,' he said. 'Between friends these little d——d accommodations ought to fly like pipe-lights.'

Fettes pocketed the money, and applauded the sentiment to the echo. 'You are a philosopher,' he cried. 'I was an ass till I knew you. You and K—— between you, by the Lord Harry! but you'll make a man of me.'

'Of course we shall,' applauded Macfarlane. 'A man? I tell you, it required a man to back me up the other morning. There are some big, brawling, forty-year-old cowards who would have turned sick at the look of the d——d thing; but not you — you kept your head. I watched you.'

'Well, and why not?' Fettes thus vaunted himself. 'It was no affair of mine. There was nothing to gain on the one side but disturbance, and on the other I could count on your gratitude, don't you see?' And he slapped his pocket till the gold pieces rang.

Macfarlane somehow felt a certain touch of alarm at these unpleasant words. He may have regretted that he had taught his young companion so successfully, but he had no time to interfere, for the other noisily continued in this boastful strain:

'The great thing is not to be afraid. Now, between you and me, I don't want to hang — that's practical; but for all **cant**[55], Macfarlane, I was born with a contempt. Hell, God, devil, right, wrong, sin, crime, and all the old gallery of curiosities — they may frighten boys, but men of the world, like you and me, despise them. Here's to the memory of Gray!'

It was by this time growing somewhat late. The gig, according to order, was brought round to the door with both lamps brightly shining, and the young men had to pay their bill and take the road. They announced that they were bound for Peebles, and drove in that direction till they were clear of the last houses of the town; then, extinguishing the lamps, returned upon their course, and followed a by-road toward Glencorse. There was no sound but that of their own passage, and the incessant, strident pouring of the rain. It was pitch

---

55. cant – hypocritical or self-righteous talk

dark; here and there a white gate or a white stone in the wall guided them for a short space across the night; but for the most part it was at a foot pace, and almost groping, that they picked their way through that **resonant**[56] blackness to their solemn and isolated destination. In the sunken woods that **traverse**[57] the neighbourhood of the burying ground the last glimmer failed them, and it became necessary to kindle a match and **reillumine**[58] one of the lanterns of the gig. Thus, under the dripping trees, and environed by huge and moving shadows, they reached the scene of their **unhallowed**[59] labours.

They were both experienced in such affairs, and powerful with the spade; and they had scarce been twenty minutes at their task before they were rewarded by a dull rattle on the coffin lid. At the same moment, Macfarlane, having hurt his hand upon a stone, flung it carelessly above his head. The grave, in which they now stood almost to the shoulders, was close to the edge of the plateau of the graveyard; and the gig lamp had been propped, the better to illuminate their labours, against a tree, and on the immediate verge of the steep bank descending to the stream. Chance had taken a sure aim with the stone. Then came a clang of broken glass; night fell upon them; sounds alternately dull and ringing announced the bounding of the lantern down the bank, and its occasional collision with the trees. A stone or two, which it had dislodged in its descent, rattled behind it into the profundities of the glen; and then silence, like night, resumed its sway; and they might bend their hearing to its utmost pitch, but naught was to be heard except the rain, now marching to the wind, now steadily falling over miles of open country.

They were so nearly at an end of their **abhorred**[60] task that they judged it wisest to complete it in the dark. The coffin was

---

56. **resonant** – deep and pulsating
57. **traverse** – cross
58. **reillumine** – relight
59. **unhallowed** – wicked
60. **abhorred** – repulsive, loathsome

exhumed[61] and broken open; the body inserted in the dripping sack and carried between them to the gig; one mounted to keep it in its place, and the other, taking the horse by the mouth, groped along by wall and bush until they reached the wider road by the Fisher's Tryst. Here was a faint, diffused radiancy, which they hailed like daylight; by that they pushed the horse to a good pace and began to rattle along merrily in the direction of the town.

They had both been wetted to the skin during their operations, and now, as the gig jumped among the deep ruts, the thing that stood propped between them fell now upon one and now upon the other. At every repetition of the horrid contact each instinctively repelled it with the greater haste; and the process, natural although it was, began to tell upon the nerves of the companions. Macfarlane made some ill-favoured jest about the farmer's wife, but it came hollowly from his lips, and was allowed to drop in silence. Still their unnatural burden bumped from side to side; and now the head would be laid, as if in confidence, upon their shoulders, and now the drenching sackcloth would flap icily about their faces. A creeping chill began to possess the soul of Fettes. He peered at the bundle, and it seemed somehow larger than at first. All over the country-side, and from every degree of distance, the farm dogs accompanied their passage with tragic **ululations**[62]; and it grew and grew upon his mind that some unnatural miracle had been accomplished, that some nameless change had befallen the dead body, and that it was in fear of their unholy burden that the dogs were howling.

'For God's sake,' said he, making a great effort to arrive at speech, 'for God's sake, let's have a light!'

Seemingly Macfarlane was affected in the same direction; for though he made no reply, he stopped the horse, passed the reins to his companion, got down, and proceeded to kindle the remaining lamp. They had by that time got no farther than

---

61. exhumed – removed from the ground, dug up
62. ululations – howls

the cross-road down to Auchenclinny. The rain still poured as though the **deluge**[63] were returning, and it was no easy matter to make a light in such a world of wet and darkness. When at last the flickering blue flame had been transferred to the wick and began to expand and clarify, and shed a wide circle of misty brightness round the gig, it became possible for the two young men to see each other and the thing they had along with them. The rain had moulded the rough sacking to the outlines of the body underneath; the head was distinct from the trunk, the shoulders plainly modelled; something at once spectral and human riveted their eyes upon the ghastly comrade of their drive.

For some time Macfarlane stood motionless, holding up the lamp. A nameless dread was swathed, like a wet sheet, about the body, and tightened the white skin upon the face of Fettes; a fear that was meaningless, a horror of what could not be, kept mounting to his brain. Another beat of the watch, and he had spoken. But his comrade **forestalled**[64] him.

'That is not a woman,' said Macfarlane, in a hushed voice.

'It was a woman when we put her in,' whispered Fettes.

'Hold that lamp,' said the other. 'I must see her face.'

And as Fettes took the lamp his companion untied the fastenings of the sack and drew down the cover from the head. The light fell very clear upon the dark, well-moulded features and smooth-shaven cheeks of a too familiar countenance, often beheld in dreams of both of these young men. A wild yell rang up into the night; each leaped from his own side into the roadway: the lamp fell, broke, and was extinguished; and the horse, terrified by this unusual commotion, bounded and went off toward Edinburgh at a gallop, bearing along with it, sole occupant of the gig, the body of the dead and long-dissected Gray.

---

63. deluge – the biblical flood (a huge and overwhelming flood)

64. forestalled – cut in before he had chance to speak

ACTIVITIES

1 THE HORROR GENRE

Objectives

- Identify key features of stories in the horror genre.
- Plan a trailer to promote a horror film.

Ever since the first stories were told, people have enjoyed being scared. Fear can be thrilling; it heightens our senses and makes us feel alive.

Word origin

The word 'horror' comes from the Latin word 'horrere', which means to shudder, tremble, [hair] stands on end.

1. In pairs, list any horror stories that you know. They could be films, books, games or TV series. Talk about why they are scary and what effect they have on you. (Look at the word origin box to help you.)

2. Read the quotations below and on page 95 about horror stories. Decide which ones you agree with and which you think apply to *Flesh and Blood*.

Horror stories always have ghosts and hauntings.

Horror stories are scary because they are full of gore, blood and violence.

Horror stories are always set at night and the weather is always bad.

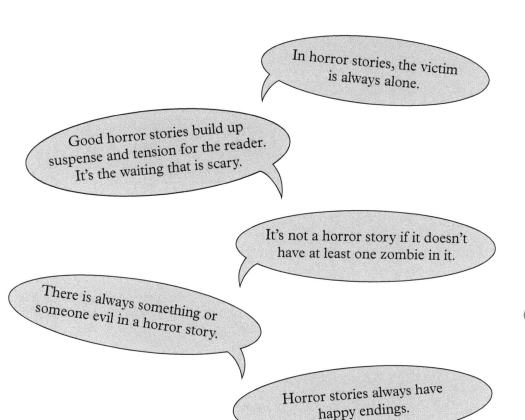

In horror stories, the victim is always alone.

Good horror stories build up suspense and tension for the reader. It's the waiting that is scary.

It's not a horror story if it doesn't have at least one zombie in it.

There is always something or someone evil in a horror story.

Horror stories always have happy endings.

3. In pairs or small groups, plan a short trailer for a film version of *Flesh and Blood*. It needs to promote the film as a horror story, so make sure you convey some of the key features of the genre in your trailer. Think about:
    ● what the opening image of the trailer will be, including what sound effects and music will be used
    ● what colours will be used in the trailer
    ● the sequence of the images and scenes
    ● a subtitle to explain the story in more detail and a voice-over to hook the reader
    ● the use of close-ups and key images.

    Remember that you want to give clues about the story, but do not give away the ending or any surprises.

Draw up a storyboard with notes to show your ideas. It might start like the one below.

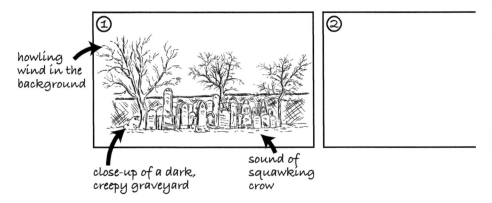

howling wind in the background

close-up of a dark, creepy graveyard

sound of squawking crow

4. When it is finished, explain your storyboard to another pair or small group, highlighting features of the horror genre.

Assessment

● **Self-assessment.** Which of the statements below do you think is most accurate about your understanding of the horror genre?

I'm not sure what features are found in horror stories.

I know some of the features that are found in horror stories.

I have a good understanding of common features found in horror stories.

● **Peer assessment.** Ask the pair or group who you explained your storyboard to to give you a rating on a scale of 1 to 5 (with 5 being the highest) about how effective they think your trailer will be. Ask them to explain their rating, saying what you did well and suggesting areas for improvement.

2 FLASHBACK

Objectives

- Understand how narrative structure can be used for effect.
- Create a story plot that uses narrative structure for effect.

Many stories start at a given point in time and then just carry on forwards. However, some writers play with the narrative structure, starting the story in the middle of the action and then taking the reader back in time to explain previous events.

1. Draw a timeline and place some markers to show when each act in *Flesh and Blood* takes place.

2. Why do you think writers use this 'flashback' technique? Choose three explanations from below and explain them in detail using evidence from *Flesh and Blood*.
   - It confuses the reader and so adds to the general mystery of the story.
   - It is a way of building suspense, so that lots of questions build up in the reader's mind and they have to read on to find out the answers.
   - It's a way of getting the reader straight into a dramatic point in the story in order to grip them.
   - It makes the story longer by telling the middle part first.
   - It's a way of building plot twists, so that the reader makes assumptions about characters and situations, only to have them overturned as they learn more about past events.

3. How does Robert Louis Stevenson use narrative structure for similar effects in his short story 'The Body Snatcher' (see pages 71–92)?

A flashback needs to be introduced by a character or another narrative device. In *Flesh and Blood* it is the ghost of Reverend Cameron, recounting past events, but the reader can also be taken back by another device, e.g. reading a letter, a diary, finding an old film, or a character travelling through time.

4. Think up an outline plot for a story that uses flashback. Use the steps below to help you.

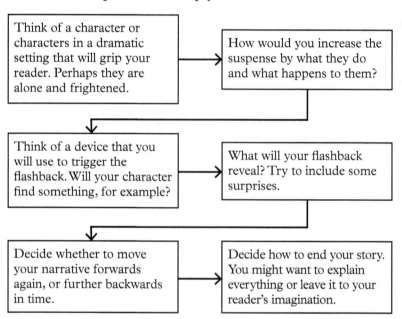

Think of a character or characters in a dramatic setting that will grip your reader. Perhaps they are alone and frightened.

→ How would you increase the suspense by what they do and what happens to them?

Think of a device that you will use to trigger the flashback. Will your character find something, for example?

→ What will your flashback reveal? Try to include some surprises.

Decide whether to move your narrative forwards again, or further backwards in time.

→ Decide how to end your story. You might want to explain everything or leave it to your reader's imagination.

ASSESSMENT

● **Teacher assessment.** Ask your teacher to comment on the strengths and weaknesses of your story outline.

● **Peer assessment.** Swap your story outline with a partner. Give them a thumbs up 👍 or thumbs down 👎 as to whether they successfully included the following aspects:
  ● good drama in the story opening and a build-up of tension
  ● a believable narrative device to trigger the flashback
  ● a satisfying explanation of the past
  ● an unexpected or surprising ending.

3 Casting Roles

Objectives

- Study characterization and how this can be conveyed effectively on stage.
- Write casting notes and explore character through role-play.

Imagine you are a casting director for a production of *Flesh and Blood*. Part of your job is to draw up casting notes for each character, including a summary of their role in the play, their personality and characteristics. You also need to suggest what they might look like and describe any mannerisms or other qualities that they might need in the role.

Read the casting notes below for Samuel Miller.

Character's name: Samuel Miller

Character's age: 17

Appearance: Good-looking but in a fairly ordinary way. He's a carpenter, so strong and physically able.

His role: Eliza's boyfriend, although her father has forbidden them to continue their relationship. He is fond of Eliza but not prepared to run away with her. When he finds out that she has made money from body snatchers he is horrified and tells her that he won't elope with her. Eliza is furious and kills him with a spade.

Character: We know from Mrs Barker that he is from 'a good family' and is honest, dislikes deceit, tends to be led by Eliza, but ultimately stands up to her when he realizes her crimes.

Additional info: His manners are not polished (he scratches his behind). He isn't particularly romantic or good with words. He doesn't think long-term and isn't particularly adventurous or imaginative. He speaks 'uncertainly' and 'hesitantly'.

1. Write your own casting notes for either Eliza or Reverend Cameron, or another character of your choice.
    - Try to include some quotations from the play to illustrate your character.
    - Think about how other characters react to them, as well as what they do and say themselves.
    - Suggest how they might look, making inferences from the text.
    - Decide if the character changes during the play and, if so, how (for example, whether the audience might be sympathetic to them at first then change their minds or vice versa).

2. Work in pairs, with one person being the casting director and the other the actor, applying for the role in the play. As part of the audition, the actor has to role-play the character, while the director asks him or her questions. Once complete, swap roles.
    - The director should ask the character questions about what they did and why, how they felt and what motivated them. They should also ask about attitudes towards the other characters.
    - The actor must reply in role, explaining their thoughts, feelings, actions and motivations. The actor should think carefully about the way their character might speak (use of pauses, tone, volume) and what facial expressions and gestures they might use. They should be in role throughout the audition.

ASSESSMENT

- **Self-assessment.** Give yourself a rating out of 5 (with 5 being highest) on how well you think you summarized your chosen character in the casting notes. Consider how well you used information given in the play, as well as your own ideas.

- **Peer assessment.** Ask your partner how well they think you portrayed your character in role. Ask them to name two aspects of the portrayal that you did well (e.g. the way you spoke, moved, gestured, or explained your actions) and one aspect that could be improved.

4 Reporting The News

● ●

Objectives

- Use appropriate language, style, presentation and level of formality in writing a non-fiction text.
- Write a news article that will appear in print and on a website.

You are a journalist who has been asked to report on the violent death of Dr Samuel Miller at a psychiatric clinic near Caldmere. There have been rumours about a patient turning violent, and some links with a murder and body-snatching episode that happened in the 1800s in the remote village of Caldmere.

Your editor thinks it sounds like a gripping story and has asked you to do some research, interview some people and to write an article that will be both printed and online. She has advised you to:

- recount recent events
- include some eye-witness accounts (e.g. from Nurse Caitlin)
- interview Emma Barker and her family (Emma is accused of the attack on Dr Miller)
- explain the links with historical events in Caldmere
- summarize what has been done to verify Emma's claims (e.g. excavations at the old vicarage in Caldmere)
- speculate on the outcome of the trial
- suggest links for the website, e.g. to the archive that dates back to the 1800s.

1. Plan your article and gather material (you will need to imagine some interviews and additional information). Then write a first draft of your article.

Use the following notes to remind you of the key features of a good news article:

Start the article with the five Ws: What? Where? When? Who? Why?

Include a suitable photo and caption.

The account must be impartial and avoid casting blame, therefore use phrases such as 'some people claim...', 'it is believed that...', 'according to eyewitness accounts...'.

Divide text into short paragraphs with a logical flow between them.

Write in Standard English, avoiding colloquialisms and slang.

Include quotations to get different viewpoints.

Use a short, attention-grabbing headline.

Include details that will interest readers, e.g. violence, gruesome detail, suggestions of supernatural events.

2. Swap your article with a partner.

Assessment

● **Peer assessment.** Ask your partner to comment on the content and structure of your draft. Does it include enough information? Do the paragraphs flow logically? Does the headline grab attention?

3. Write a final draft of your article, bearing in mind your partner's comments. Proofread your text for grammar, punctuation and spelling mistakes, using a dictionary if necessary. Check that you have used a variety of sentence types to keep the text lively. Highlight or underline any hyperlinks that you have included for the online version.

If possible, present your article as a Word document, so that it can be printed out and displayed.

Assessment

● **Teacher assessment.** Ask your teacher to act as 'Editor' and to comment on your article, identifying what you have done well and any areas that need further work. In particular, ask him or her to suggest where you could have been more concise. News articles sometimes have to be cut to fit into the space available.

5 Improvising A New Scene

Objectives

- Use role-play to explore events, characters and possible alternative outcomes in plot.
- Improvise a new scene between two characters.

In Act 2 Scene 4, Samuel arrives at the graveyard to meet Eliza but he tells her: 'I was nearly spotted by your father! He was flying down the hill so fast he nearly ran straight into me. I just had time to jump behind a tree.'

Imagine that Samuel didn't hide from Reverend Cameron. In pairs, improvise a new scene where they meet. Follow the steps below.

1. Allocate roles. Then on your own, think carefully about:
   - how your character would greet the other one
   - how your character feels and what he is planning to do
   - whether you will tell the truth to the other character
   - whether your character is likely to quiz the other one, or whether he will be too preoccupied to ask questions
   - what your character's attitude is towards the other character and how you would convey this in the scene
   - the possible outcome of the scene and what may happen next.

2. In order to get into role, jot down a few adjectives to describe your character and their mood. Alternatively, choose the most suitable from the selection below.

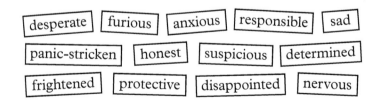

desperate	furious	anxious	responsible	sad
panic-stricken	honest	suspicious	determined
frightened	protective	disappointed	nervous

3. Decide how you will convey your character's mood and personality through the way that you act. How will you move? How will you speak? What will be your facial expressions and gestures? How will you use pauses, volume and intonation to add impact to what you say? Will you have any props or wear anything that might affect how you portray your character?

4. Re-read your character's last speeches before this improvised scene to help you get into role. You might also want to skim through the last scene so that your new scene flows on smoothly from the most recent action.

5. Improvise your scene in front of an audience (another pair, a group or the whole class). Try to remain in character throughout, reacting to what the other character says and does in a credible manner. Allow the scene to develop as naturally as possible, even if it means that the rest of the story may have a different outcome to the existing one.

6. After your improvised scene, discuss whether it would change the outcome of the play and how. Do you think the addition of this scene would make the play more or less exciting?

ASSESSMENT

- **Peer assessment.** Ask your audience to comment on whether you did the following:
  - remained in character throughout the scene
  - behaved in a way that was credible for that character
  - responded to the other character in a believable way
  - conveyed your character effectively, through what you said, how you said it and how you moved.

- **Teacher assessment.** Ask your teacher to choose one improvisation from the class that he or she felt was particularly effective and to explain why.

6 An Alternative Interpretation

Objectives

- Understand how interpretations of characters and plays can vary, depending on a director's choices.
- Explore an alternative interpretation of Eliza through adapting scenes and writing a diary extract.

A director decides how to interpret a play by choosing how and what they emphasize in the characters, setting and plot. For example, one director might present a king who murders his rivals as an evil, paranoid tyrant, whereas another director might present this king as an insecure victim, who has to keep one step ahead of his evil courtiers who are plotting against him.

If you were a director who wanted to portray Eliza in a more sympathetic way, how would you do this? Look at the suggestions below.

I would make the audience feel sorry for her by emphasizing that her mother has just died, which explains her temper and moodiness.

I would make her father seem less kind. He could be possessive over Eliza and treat her badly.

I would make Samuel seem to be more interested in her money, rather than her company.

I would make Eliza more of a role model for independence and initiative, showing business enterprise and determination to break out of a traditional role.

I would make Emma seem more unpleasant and the Barker twins more mean, so the audience feel that Eliza is right to want 'justice'.

1. In pairs or small groups, choose one of these suggestions and decide how you would perform a particular scene to convey your interpretation. Think about:
   - whether you would change any of the actual script (words that are said)
   - how the actors would say their words and move, and react to each other to convey your interpretation (gestures, facial expressions, tones of voice)
   - whether you would introduce any other details to reinforce your interpretation, e.g. a spiteful act by one of the Barker twins, or physical cruelty from her father or Samuel.

2. Rehearse and then perform your scene in front of an audience.

ASSESSMENT

- **Peer assessment.** Ask your audience whether they felt any differently towards Eliza after seeing your scene and, if so, why. Ask them to suggest any improvement to the scene, for example whether there was anything that they didn't quite understand or whether a character didn't seem believable.

3. One way to influence an audience's impression of a character is to reveal more about that character's thoughts and feelings. Imagine Eliza's old diary is discovered. Write an entry which you think will make Eliza a more likeable character and make the audience sympathize with her more.

Use some of the sentence starters below if you wish.

June 10th 1825

It's been another difficult day. I tried hard to …

Father has been in an awful temper and …

I'm so lonely and miss Mother so much that …

I'm not just going to lead the life that everyone wants me to …

Those twins have been getting me into trouble again …

Remember that Eliza is writing in the 1800s, so do not include any anachronisms (things that belong to a different time), such as watching TV, using a mobile or eating a pizza!

ASSESSMENT

- **Self-assessment.** Give yourself a rating on a scale of 1 to 5 (with 5 being the highest) on how well you did the following:
  - contributed to the group discussion about how to portray Eliza more sympathetically
  - kept in role during your scene
  - showed Eliza in a sympathetic light in your diary extract.

7 Body-Snatching: Medical Necessity Or Outrageous Crime?

● ●

> **Objectives**
>
> ● Explore the moral issues surrounding the supply of bodies for anatomy study.
> ● Participate in a debate about whether body-snatching was an excusable crime.

Re-read the conversation between Fettes and MacFarlane in Act 2 Scene 4 about body-snatching. MacFarlane calls it 'an honourable cause' and uses humour to try to ease the tension, but Fettes is troubled by his conscience.

In the early 1800s, body-snatching was common because the law stated that only the bodies of executed criminals could be used for dissection in anatomy lessons in medical schools. The need for bodies was greater than the supply, so grave-robbing became commonplace. The authorities were aware of the shortfall and often turned a blind eye to this common practice, although it was illegal.

Step 1
Split into two groups: those who feel that body-snatching was entirely wrong; and those who feel that body-snatching was excusable because of medical necessity.

Step 2
Appoint an impartial chairperson who will have authority to say who can speak when.

Step 3
Each group should appoint a spokesperson to represent their views.

FLESH AND BLOOD ACTIVITIES

Step 4

Each group needs to research and discuss their viewpoint, and draw up a list of arguments to support it. They should also try to anticipate what their opponents might say and think of counter-arguments. Some areas to explore are shown in the boxes below and opposite. Each group should ensure that:

● everyone has an opportunity to express his or her ideas

● everyone listens to what is said and responds to it.

Step 5

Each speaker presents their group's viewpoint. He or she might find it useful to have notes to refer to during the presentation.

Step 6

The chairperson 'opens the floor' to other viewpoints – letting everyone have their say.

Step 7

A vote is taken. The side with the most votes wins.

Against body-snatching – questions to consider:

● How would families have felt if they knew recently dead relatives had been dissected?

● Are we sure that there is no conscious life after death?

● How would it conflict with religious beliefs?

● Could medical students have used fake bodies instead?

● Could body-snatching lead to murder? (It did in the case of William Burke and William Hare, who murdered victims before selling their bodies to medical schools.)

Sympathy for body-snatching – questions to consider:

- How else could students learn about the human body?

- How else could students gain experience of surgery, such as amputations?

- What better use is there for a dead body?

- Does the fact that the authorities tolerated it to an extent show that the benefits outweighed the disadvantages?

- Who suffered, if the body-snatching was never discovered?

William Burke and William Hare murdered their victims before supplying them to Doctor Robert Knox to dissect at the Edinburgh Medical School in the 1820s. Burke was hanged for his crimes. Hare escaped punishment because he testified against Burke.

Assessment

- **Self-assessment.** Consider how well you worked in the group. Did you:
    - listen carefully to what others said?
    - respond to what others said?
    - present your own views effectively?

- **Teacher assessment.** Invite your teacher to name two people who contributed to the discussion effectively and to comment on why their contributions were successful.

FURTHER ACTIVITIES

1. Find out more about body-snatching in the 1800s and how people tried to guard against it.

2. Read another horror story by Robert Louis Stevenson, such as *Dr Jekyll and Mr Hyde*, or one of his supernatural short stories, such as 'Olalla'.

3. Write a ten-question quiz to test your partner's knowledge about the play *Flesh and Blood*. Include questions about its setting, its links with historical stories, some of the characters and the plot.

4. As an extended writing task, complete the story that you planned on pages 97–98.

5. Discuss the title of the play *Flesh and Blood*. What are its connotations? Suggest an alternative title and explain why you think it is suitable.

6. Plan an alternative Act 4, giving the playscript a different outcome. Try to include a 'twist' to surprise the reader or leave a question in the reader's mind.